Runaway
America

Runaway America

U.S. JOBS AND FACTORIES ON THE MOVE

Harry Browne & Beth Sims

PUBLISHED BY THE RESOURCE CENTER PRESS

Albuquerque, New Mexico

Resource Center Press
Box 4506/ Albuquerque, New Mexico 87196

ISBN: 0-911213-43-0

Library of Congress Catalog Card Number: 93-78247

Acknowledgments

This book could not have been produced without the insights and efforts of many people besides the two who put it on paper and received credit on the cover. Our thanks go first of all to the colleagues and activists who generously took time out of crowded schedules to share their experiences and offer valuable comments on our discussion of runaways, international economic integration, and community responses. We discussed these issues with far too many knowledgeable people to list them all here, but several must be singled out for the quality of their feedback and the good nature with which they accepted our repeated phone calls. These include Jim Benn, Jeremy Brecher, Steven Deutsch, Pharis Harvey, Thea Lee, Staughton Lynd, and David Ranney. Other development specialists and community and labor activists who were particularly helpful include Sonia Angell, Randy Barber, Bob Becker, Lynn Feekin, Karen Hansen-Kuhn, Seymour Melman, Lauren Rothfarb, Harley Shaiken, Greg Tarpinian, and Bill Troy.

A book with an activist agenda, like this one, inevitably draws on the work of other organizations that are committed to social change. We are grateful to a number of unions for their independent efforts to trace runaway plants and for their assistance with our research. The ACTWU, AFL-CIO, IBEW, IUE, UAW, and UE stand out in this regard. Likewise, the efforts of organizations like the Federation for Industrial Retention and Renewal, the Midwest Center for Labor Research, and the International Labor Rights Education and Research Fund provide models for new development paths that will serve human needs. The staffs at these organizations were especially helpful during our research on feasible responses to the process of globalization and the runaway phenomenon. Our research also depended on the work of investigative reporters across the country who have penetrated the corporate public relations fog that often surrounds decisions to relocate jobs abroad.

As always, our co-workers at the Resource Center provided crucial support to our work. Our thanks go especially to Jerry Harvey, whose efforts to collect data laid the foundation for our runaways list and demonstrated both tremendous patience and great initiative; Laura Sheridan and Jodi Gibson, whose research assistance was essential to confirming or ruling out suspected runaway plants; intern Arin Dunn, for his work on the resources list and for the many hours he spent doing interviews with activists; and John Hawley, for his painstaking work on design and production. A special word of thanks is reserved for Tom Barry, for his provocative criticisms, editorial insights, and encouragement.

Contents

Winners and Losers in the Global Economy

GLOBALIZATION IS CHANGING the face of the country. Across the United States, manufacturing plants and other businesses are closing down while their parent corporations open or expand operations abroad. Jobs once held by U.S. workers at decent wages are being exported. In the meantime, the daily wages that U.S. corporations are paying their new foreign employees would barely pay for the burger, fries, and coke that many displaced workers in the United States are now forced to sell for a living.

Nobody said competing in the international economy would be easy. But as the global economic position of the United States declines and as U.S. corporations enhance competitiveness by slashing costs, working people and their communities are footing the bill. These experiences are not just confined to the United States, however, and *Runaway America* is not just about the countries of North America. Affecting any country and any community that is somehow tied into the international economy, the processes described in this book are global in scope and have serious repercussions on the welfare of people everywhere. Workers and communities around the world are paying a disproportionate share of the burden of globalization because the structure of the global economy puts them at a disadvantage. Although money, technology, and information move across the world as if national boundaries do not exist, workers and their communities are stuck. Not only confined by territory and immigration restrictions, they are also bound by national laws and international agreements—domestic policies and practices that restrict union organizing, for example, or trade accords that fail to protect worker and community rights.

In contrast, transnational corporations (TNCs) can pull up stakes and travel the world looking for the most favorable conditions, the lowest costs, the fewest regulations, the most compliant labor. This capacity gives TNCs a powerful advantage over those who need to make a daily living in this world. In addition, by adding a huge reserve of international workers to the pool of available labor, globalization itself has undermined the position of workers everywhere.

In the global economy, labor, as well as local, regional, and national governments, must compete with international counterparts to encourage transnational employers to set up shop in their communities or to keep established plants from leaving. The effect has been a downward slide of wages and living conditions as nations and corporations "discipline" their labor forces in the competition for investment capital and global market shares. Workers themselves have given up hard-won rights and material benefits obtained through years of organizing efforts and social reforms. Making matters worse, deindustrialization—the decline of manufacturing industries—is doing its part to sap the developed countries of their productive base as investment in plant equipment and training plunges.

The economic uncertainty that results from these trends is taking its toll. Working people and their communities are losing the control they thought they had over their economic futures. The postwar prosperity boom that seemed to promise so much in the way of upward mobility, leisure time, and economic security has nearly gone bust. These trends are not confined to the United States. Globalization means that corporations are increasingly footloose and workers in countries like Mexico who may get hired to work at a plant once based in the United States cannot count on their jobs either. Other low-wage sites threaten them, just as they threaten U.S. workers, fueling the competition to undercut wages and hack away at regulations that might enforce corporate accountability.

Concerned by these circumstances and their human repercussions, we decided to examine closely the phenomenon of globalization and to explore some alternatives to the problems it presents for workers and communities. Using the United States and Mexico as examples of a worldwide process, we have focused especially on runaway plants—those companies that relocate operations in other countries, often exporting their products and services back to the U.S. market unimpeded.[1]

In the course of our research, we have compiled the most comprehensive list to date of specific plants that have shipped some or all of their production to Mexico. Numbering more than 250 confirmed sites, this list shows the geographic and industrial breadth of the runaway phenomenon (see Appendix A). Although U.S. companies have "run away" to a multitude of low-wage export-processing zones across the globe, nowhere has the phenomenon been more visible than right across the border. Since the 1960s hundreds of manufacturers and service providers have left for Mexico, leaving behind more than 100,000 U.S. workers and their communities.

Why do these corporations move jobs to foreign locations? In our research on Mexico, we have identified several major incentives. Although our focus is on Mexico, these same incentives underlie relocations to other destinations as well. Most corporations move or threaten to move because:

- wages are lower and benefits fewer;
- the work force is less likely to be organized; if it is organized, it is less likely to be assertive;
- management can exert clear control over the work process, with few or no restrictions on hiring, firing, or reassigning workers;
- relocating some operations can force concessions from workers who remain at other operations in the United States;
- workplace health and safety regulations are less stringent or poorly enforced; and
- the costs of protecting the environment and community health and safety are lower due to weak or poorly enforced regulations.

This attempt to study runaways and the effects of globalization in the United States and Mexico comes at a crucial time. International trade and investment issues have long been important to the economic security of workers and communities and to the economic health of the nation. For the most part, however, these issues have not drawn much interest from the public or policymakers, even in terms of their domestic effects. On an international scale, the impacts of trade, investment, and other components of globalization on foreign workers and communities have received still less attention.

But the potential for a North American Free Trade Agreement (NAFTA) has prompted widespread interest and concern. If approved by the legislatures in the signatory countries, NAFTA will join Canada, Mexico, and the United States in a regional free trade area. As negotiated, NAFTA will eliminate all tariffs and import quotas within fifteen years. Nontariff barriers to free trade, such as product safety standards, could also be challenged under the accord. NAFTA will facilitate the flow of goods and services in the region, but it will also encourage increased cross-border investment by requiring that most North American investors be given the same rights and opportunities as domestic investors.

By stimulating increased cross-border investment and by tightly linking the economies of the United States and Mexico, NAFTA threatens to accelerate the movement of U.S. plants to Mexico. This possibility touched a raw nerve in many U.S. communities already tested by plant closures and fearful of more. It also raised concerns among Mexican labor and community activists who fear that their country would be used merely to provide a cheap and expendable work force to boost the corporate earnings of U.S. TNCs and powerful Mexican businesses. The trade agreement has therefore awakened debate about the economic processes underlying globalization, runaways, and associated processes like deindustrialization.

It will be clear that this book has a "point of view" on matters like these. It would be surprising, given the controversiality and importance of the subject, if it did not. We find ourselves in the middle of a heated debate that will determine what path this country and this continent will take as global economic integration proceeds. NAFTA is the current focus of that debate, but the trade agreement is just one element of a package of economic policies and institutions that are being structured to give more freedom to corporations and less democratic decisionmaking power to the workers and communities of the world.

The multilateral General Agreement on Tariffs and Trade (GATT), for example, is being renegotiated in ways that threaten to undermine environmental and consumer safety and health regulations that are tougher than international minimums. In fact, strict standards for protecting quality-of-life issues like labor rights, the environment, and consumer safety are being assaulted as "restraints" on trade. Similarly, programs like the Enterprise for the Americas Initiative, proposed by the Bush administration, and the mounting wave of free trade proposals throughout the world are unlikely to result in equitable, sustainable development.[2] In deference to the "neoliberal" economic theories that currently hold sway among policymakers—and among the moneyed interests that keep them in office—these initiatives are being set up to free corporations and capital to the maximum extent possible. As currently envisioned, they would undermine existing regulations designed to protect labor and the environment, while making it increasingly difficult to enact strict labor and environmental regulations in the future. Through deregulation and other mechanisms, such as privatization, these programs will give increasing power over national economic issues to corporate elites rather than elected representatives. Along with the downward pressure on wages and working conditions that results from an increasingly global work force and community competition for investment, these programs will threaten equity, democracy, and sustainability worldwide.

We hope that this book will contribute to the debate over how globalization and economic integration will be structured so that these obstacles to democracy and economic security can be overcome. The first chapter gives a brief overview of globalization since World War II. One section in this chapter explores the growth of maquiladora industries along the U.S.-Mexico border as the forerunner to the economic integration that is occurring today. Chapter 1 also reviews the human dimensions of the runaway process, deindustrialization, and economic restructuring in the United States.

Chapter 2 describes the movement of U.S. jobs and factories to other locations, using runaways to Mexico as examples of a global process. Case studies drawn from our list of runaways to Mexico are used to illustrate the reasons behind corporate decisions to cut back or close operations in the United States and relocate them abroad.

Chapter 3 addresses the free-market economic theories often used to downplay the significance of plant closings and to support trade agreements that enhance corporate freedom. The chapter evaluates the increasingly common argument that manufacturing jobs will return to high-wage countries as such factors as worker training, rapidly changing technologies, and tighter linkages among design, production, and marketing grow in importance.

The final chapter explores ways for workers and communities to respond to globalization, runaways, and deindustrialization by reclaiming control over economic decisionmaking. Global economic integration is not an independent force following a predestined path. The crucial issue for communities, workers, environmentalists, and other concerned citizens is to come to grips with the process and effects of globalization so that it can be regulated and shaped to meet the needs of people and communities.

Three appendices conclude the book. Appendix A is our list of U.S. corporations that have relocated to Mexico. The runaways are organized first by state and then alphabetically, according to the corporation's name, within each state. Appendix B describes the methodology used to determine which U.S. corporations to include in our list of runaways. Appendix C includes an extensive list of publications, organizations, and other resources to provide activists and researchers with information and assistance as they explore the effects of globalization and devise alternatives.

Globalization and the U.S. Economy

UNDERSTANDING THE SCOPE OF THE RUN-away problem means understanding globalization. Since the end of World War II, national economies around the world have become increasingly integrated into a global economy. A profound shift in the organization of manufacturing is to a large degree behind this integration. Advances in telecommunications, information processing, and transportation technology have made it possible to coordinate extremely complex manufacturing processes—from product design and investment financing to inventory management and marketing—in several countries simultaneously. In an attempt to make their companies more efficient, corporations have "rationalized" their operations by splitting up portions of their production chains and relocating the various links to countries with lower labor costs, more competitive suppliers, cheaper natural resources, or more favorable government policies. Separated by international borders, language, and culture, groups of workers around the world who work for the same company function as employees in a global factory. They produce for the same markets with largely the same technology, answer to the same executives, and generate dividends for the same shareholders.

Besides revolutionary changes in technology, the international economy is made possible by financial and banking networks that span the globe and facilitate trade, investment, and other economic relationships. Also important is an increasingly centralized international economic system, with an overarching economic regime that sets the rules for international economic relations. Formalized in a variety of economic agreements and institutions constructed by the postwar capitalist powers, but dominated by the United States, this economic regime is designed to give businesses as much freedom as possible to move money, jobs, and other resources to seek the most profit.

The 1944 Bretton Woods Agreement, for example, created an international economic system built on the principle of maximum freedom for capital: free trade, free movement of capital, and free exchange of currencies.[1] Two institutions created under the agreement, the International Monetary Fund and the World Bank, have conditioned much of their support to developing countries since the early 1980s on the recipient's close adherence to free-market principles. Another outgrowth of Bretton Woods, the General Agreement on Tariffs and Trade (GATT), established rules for the international market aimed at eliminating many restrictions on trade and investment.

Over time, these institutions accelerated the spread of global capitalism by reducing barriers to the free movement of capital, goods, and services. Moreover, such agreements have served as levers to apply global pressure on governments to reduce or eliminate restrictions on businesses in such areas as environmental, labor, and consumer protection. During the recent Uruguay Round of negotiations to update GATT, for example, the U.S. negotiating team proposed policies that could make regulations for environmental and consumer protection that exceed international ceilings vulnerable to assault as unfair trade practices.[2] Other policies endangered during the talks included those intended to safeguard natural resources and local markets. New regional trade agreements, like the hotly debated NAFTA, will dismantle even more trade and investment barriers, allowing corporations in the signatory countries to shuttle the continent ever more freely.

Growth of Runaways

One of the worst byproducts of the global factory and the global harmonization of trade and investment rules is the runaway plant.

Runaways are a relatively new phenomenon. In the 1950s a number of visionary corporate managers saw that freer trade flows and the revolutions in communications and transportation meant access not just to foreign consumer markets but also to vast low-paid labor markets. Led by the electronics and apparel industries, these managers set up labor-intensive facilities in Asia, the Caribbean, and Mexico. Opening new investment sites abroad would simply be corporate expansion if existing enterprises in the United States were kept running at normal capacity. Instead, by the mid-1960s, TNCs began cutting back on personnel or closing down operations at U.S. plants in order to set up shop where costs were lower for one aspect or another of the production process.

The decision of these corporations to move abroad made sense given the structure of the international economy. Although the Bretton Woods system was set up according to free-market principles, the rules agreed upon by the participants were always applied unevenly in practice. Thus, although the U.S. market has been comparatively open since World War II, markets abroad have frequently been shielded by protectionist government policies. This dichotomy was tolerable during the first decade or so after World War II, when U.S. corporations clearly dominated global markets with superior, reasonably priced products. But as Europe and Japan rebuilt and as Asian governments launched comprehensive industrial development programs, manufacturers in this country found themselves competing with foreign firms that used far cheaper labor, received government subsidies, or enjoyed home markets that were not open to U.S. products. Under these conditions, relocation abroad was—and is—an understandable reaction to international competition, even though it does nothing to ensure competitiveness or economic security in the long run.[3]

Over the years the number of U.S. plants that have pulled up roots and headed abroad has ballooned. Mexico is only one of their destinations. The country's proximity and the amount of U.S. investment there make it a prime example for study, but U.S. corporations have shipped jobs to countries around the globe. From El Salvador to Czechoslovakia, from Haiti to Malaysia, the world has become a global factory for U.S. transnational corporations (see Table 1.1).

The growth of runaways as a major problem in the United States has been closely associated with the decline of industrial production, a process known as deindustrialization.[4] Instead of plowing profits back into existing plants or investing in new U.S. manufacturing operations to spur innovation, upgrade equipment and worker skills, and thus boost productivity, many corporations since the 1960s have chosen instead to maximize profit rates by other means. Sometimes they have moved production to sites where operating costs would be lower, thus becoming runaways.[5] Speculative investments and acquisitions also contribute to deindustrialization by diverting funds that might otherwise be used to upgrade and modernize current plants.

For whatever reason disinvestment and deindustrialization occur, they erode the competitiveness of U.S. industries and have profoundly negative effects on the economic security of workers and

TABLE 1.1 ■ SEE WHERE THEY RUN: TOP LOCATIONS FOR U.S. PRODUCTION SHARING IN 1991[§]

COUNTRY	AMOUNT
Mexico	$7,254,872,600
Canada	2,517,651,700
Dominican Republic	643,460,700
Central America	556,616,300
Japan	533,911,200
Malaysia	531,903,400
South Korea	496,175,400
All Others	1,982,607,600
Total	14,517,198,600

[§] These figures represent the duty-free value of imports into the United States under the Harmonized Tariff Schedule 9802 (HTS 9802). Under this U.S. tariff law, firms are allowed to import goods without paying duties on any U.S.-made components or materials used to produce the goods. Firms in the United States that share production with affiliates or contractors abroad bring their products back into the United States under HTS 9802. These totals provide a reasonable picture of the most popular sites for U.S. production sharing and, by extrapolation, the most common destinations for U.S. runaways.

SOURCE: U.S. Census Bureau, *IM-146-A Report* (Washington, DC: Government Printing Office, 1992).

communities. Major sectors of the U.S. economy are closing down. The structure of the economy is changing from one that used to support a range of decent-paying jobs with reasonable benefits to one that offers mostly low-wage, no-benefits employment in the service sector. During the 1950s, nearly a third of all U.S. workers were employed in manufacturing. By the 1980s only 20 percent had such jobs. In the early 1990s the figure had slipped to 17 percent and was still falling.[6] In addition, the share of the gross domestic product provided by manufacturing has also declined, especially since 1979.[7]

Labor-intensive industries like electronics assembly and apparel were the first to experience the shift of jobs abroad. Increasingly, however, runaways are likely to be capital-intensive operations, or even firms in the service sector. This change in the composition of industries that are moving abroad is especially clear in Mexico, where the sector known as the maquiladoras has expanded to include a wider range of high-value production (see Figure 1.1).

The decline in U.S. manufacturing jobs, with all its ill consequences for U.S. workers, has not meant a crisis for many of the U.S. corporations involved in such manufacturing. Statistics show that U.S. manufacturers capable of transnationalizing have adapted to global competition by doing so. Although the share of world manufactured exports produced in the *United States* dropped from 17.1 percent in 1966 to 13.4 percent in 1985, the share of global production held by U.S.-owned corporations actually increased from 17.3 percent to 18.3 percent. The corporations had not lost business or gone under. They had simply shifted much of their production to foreign subsidiaries.[8]

The Human Dimension

The logic of the globalization process puts the workers, communities, and governments of the world in direct competition for a limited pool of capital and technology. The rivalries that are stimulated—in tandem with national policies and international agreements that are biased against workers, the environment, and public health and safety—exert a downward tug on living and working conditions around the world. As cash-starved governments fight to offer the lowest paid and most compliant work forces, for instance, they often resort to repressing labor and ignoring national laws on minimum wages and working conditions. A. Sivanandan, the direc-

FIGURE 1.1 ■ **MAQUILA EMPLOYMENT BY ECONOMIC SECTOR, 1979–1991**

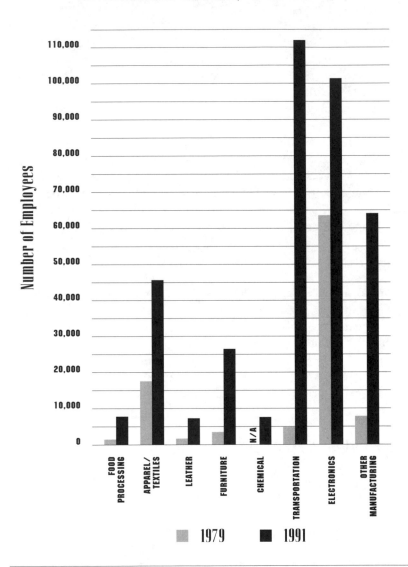

1979   1991

SOURCES: 1979 statistics from Instituto Nacional para Estadística, Geografía e Informática (INEGI), cited in Leslie Sklair, *Assembling for Development: The Maquila Industry in Mexico and the United States* (Winchester, MA: Unwin Hyman, 1989), p. 70. 1991 statistics from American Chamber of Commerce, *Review of Trade and Industry Including Maquiladora Newsletter*, 2d Quarter, 1992, p. 13

tor of London's Institute of Race Relations, offered a grim description of the process:

> The governments of the [underdeveloped countries], desperate not for development as such but the end to the unemployment that threatens their regimes, enter into a Dutch auction with each other, offering the multinational corporations cheaper and cheaper labour, de-unionized labour, captive labour, female labour and child labour—by removing whatever labour laws, whatever trade union rights have been gained in the past from at least that part of the country . . . which foreign capital chooses for its own.[9]

In most cases the shift to new, globally oriented plants enabled corporations to weaken the grip of labor unions and increase managerial control over the organization of work. Threats of relocation aimed at unionists and other workers in the United States are frequently used to extract concessions in terms of wage and benefits packages, work conditions, hours of work, job classifications, and organizing efforts.[10] In addition to eroding standards for worker protection, unions themselves have been discredited, dismantled, and destroyed both in the United States and abroad.[11]

Negative spinoffs of deindustrialization and the runaway phenomenon (such as the decline of unionism, eroding standards for environmental and consumer protections, and decay of infrastructure) result only in part from the impersonal actions of international economic forces. In fact, as instruments such as GATT illustrate, even seemingly "natural" forces like international economics are shaped by the political choices of governments and influential private actors. But problems like these also stem from the domestic policies of national governments. When, for instance, the administration of President Ronald Reagan moved to crush the air traffic controllers union in the early 1980s, the move was not aimed at transforming the global economy or the position of the United States in it. Instead the U.S. president acted as the leader of a coalition of conservative politicians, economists, and interest groups who were employing the "discipline of the whip" against U.S. labor.[12] From trickle-down economics to the deregulation frenzy of the 1980s, U.S. domestic politics savaged labor, the working poor, the middle class, and the environment. In interaction with the forces of globalization, such policies contribute to the runaway phenomenon and to its negative impacts on U.S. workers.[13]

Pressure on Workers and Communities

The price tag attached to deindustrialization and the runaway phenomenon is an expensive one. Although corporations that "run away" may find their own profits climbing, the communities and workers they leave behind are often tossed into economic catastrophe. When the factory gates are padlocked, the economic and social repercussions ripple throughout affected communities. The loss of wages and benefits is traumatic enough, but displaced workers often also lose their homes, cars, and savings. Social problems like alcoholism, domestic violence, divorce, and crime increase. Other local and regional businesses feel the pinch, too, and may even go under themselves if enough of their customers lose significant buying power.[14] Although demands on social services rise due to increased unemployment, local governments suffer lost revenue from plant closures, both from corporate taxes and from taxes formerly paid by plant employees.

DYING FOR A JOB

Plant closures and layoffs carry a prohibitive cost for many of the workers who lose their jobs, as well as the communities in which they live. From substance abuse to domestic violence, from heart disease to suicide, the toll is severe.

Each 1-percent increase in the unemployment rate that is sustained over a period of six years is associated with:

- 37,000 total deaths
- 920 suicides
- 650 homicides
- 500 deaths from cirrhosis of the liver
- 4,000 admissions to state mental health hospitals
- 3,300 admissions to state prisons

SOURCE: Harvey Brenner, "Estimating the Social Costs of National Economic Policy: Implications for Mental and Physical Health and Clinical Aggression" (Report prepared for the Joint Economic Committee, U.S. Congress, Washington, DC: Government Printing Office, 1976), cited in Barry Bluestone and Bennett Harrison, *The Deindustrialization of America: Plant Closings, Community Abandonment, and the Dismantling of Basic Industry* (New York: Basic Books, 1982), p. 65.

The most profound evidence of deindustrialization and decline in the United States is seen in the slide in middle-class living standards and the climb in the poverty rate. These problems are not only the result of globalization, of course. Through tax policies, cutbacks in social programs, deregulation, union-busting efforts, inadequate funding for watchdog agencies, and similar initiatives, the Reagan and Bush administrations undermined the poor and the middle class, while shifting income upward to the wealthy[15] (see Figure 1.2). In addition, corporate raiding, leveraged buyouts, corporate restructuring, and other get-rich-and-get-out schemes have led to plant closures and layoffs across the country, in part because government policies reward such adventurism. Globalization itself—both because it has led to a re-

FIGURE 1.2 ■ FAMILY INCOME GROWTH, 1980–1990

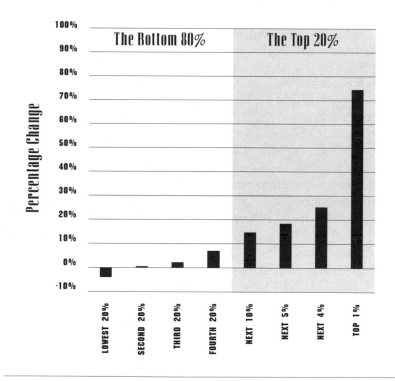

SOURCE: Lawrence Mishel and David M. Frankel, *The State of Working America 1990-91* (Armonk, NY: M.E. Sharpe Inc., 1991), p. 24.

structuring of the U.S. economy and because it poses the threat of plant relocation and job loss—also eats away at income levels for the majority of workers in the economy. Whether through concessions on wages and benefits or through outright job loss due to plant relocation, the downward pressure on living conditions is severe.

This slide in living standards is evident in statistics on median family income level.[16] The postwar prosperity that more than doubled the median family income from $14,741 in 1947 to $31,144 in 1973 has slowed to the point that a middle-class lifestyle is increasingly difficult to maintain.[17] Worse, it is further out of reach than ever for the least privileged in society: minorities, women, and the working poor. Home ownership, a decent education, reliable health care, adequate leisure time—aspirations that used to be considered part of the middle-class "American dream"—are increasingly difficult to obtain for ever-larger segments of the U.S. public. Income levels are growing too slowly to make these dreams come true. From 1979 to 1989, the median family income grew by only $1,369, a change of a mere 0.4 percent per year, compared to rates more than twice that from 1973 to 1979. Moreover, this rate of growth was only one-seventh the rate of income growth over the postwar years prior to 1973[18] (see Figure 1.3). Even more dismally, the income growth that did occur came not from pay increases but from putting more family members to work, and by working more hours each week and more weeks each year.[19]

It is not that the economy is not growing. It is, but too sluggishly to provide enough good jobs for the new workers entering the labor force—by choice or by necessity—each year. Most of the jobs that are being created are low-paid with few benefits. Job growth is taking place primarily in the retail and service sectors, while those sectors that used to provide the majority of "middle-class" wages in this country—manufacturing and construction, for instance—have lost jobs over the years, often to runaways (see Figure 1.4). In fact, the 500 largest U.S. industrial companies added no new U.S. jobs between 1975 and 1990, and their share of the civilian labor force slipped from 17 percent to less than 10 percent during that time.[20]

By the late 1980s millions of workers who had formed the backbone of the middle class had been thrown out of work by plant shutdowns. Government studies indicated that more than half of all "displaced" workers were still unemployed six months after being laid off. Even among workers who succeeded in regaining employment, more had moved down the pay scale in taking their new positions than had moved up. On average, displaced workers suffered real earnings losses of 10 to 15 percent.[21]

Laid-off workers were not the only ones seeing their salaries drop. New entrants to the work force competed with those experienced workers whose jobs had been eliminated. And although the economy was generating new jobs, few of these paid a family wage. From 1979 to 1987, 21.2 million more jobs were created than had been lost. But over half of the new positions paid less than the poverty line for a family of four—$13,400 per year—and only 7.6 percent paid more than the median annual salary of $26,800.[22] Real manufacturing wages in the United States declined 5 to 10 percent even as labor productivity increased.[23] Wages in other non-supervisory positions decreased as well, especially in the service sector (see Figure 1.5). Millions of workers were able to keep their jobs only by agreeing to employers' demands for wage and benefit cuts or, in nonunion settings, by implicitly accepting them. These trends have meant more work and less pay for the average

FIGURE 1.3 ■ MEDIAN FAMILY INCOME, 1967–1989

SOURCE: Lawrence Mishel and David M. Frankel, *The State of Working America 1990-91* (Armonk, NY: M.E. Sharpe Inc., 1991), p. 14.

FIGURE 1.4 ■ U.S. EMPLOYMENT BY SECTOR, 1950–1992
(in thousands of jobs)

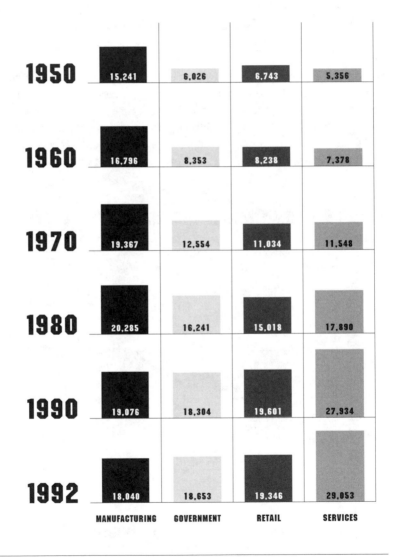

	MANUFACTURING	GOVERNMENT	RETAIL	SERVICES
1950	15,241	6,026	6,743	5,356
1960	16,796	8,353	8,238	7,378
1970	19,367	12,554	11,034	11,548
1980	20,285	16,241	15,018	17,890
1990	19,076	18,304	19,601	27,934
1992	18,040	18,653	19,346	29,053

SOURCE: Figures provided by the U.S. Bureau of Labor Statistics.

worker, a widening income gap between the top 20 percent of households and everyone else, and fewer opportunities for anyone without postsecondary education.

Race to the Border

For a microcosm of the global runaway phenomenon, we need only look as far as the U.S.-Mexico border. There the promotion of export-oriented assembly plants—known as maquiladoras—represented the first step toward the integration of Mexico into the U.S. manufacturing base. That integration, based primarily on production sharing, stimulated runaways and deindustrialization in the United States while failing to improve the living conditions of work-

FIGURE 1.5 ■ **EARNINGS GROWTH FOR PRODUCTION WORKERS, 1947–1989**

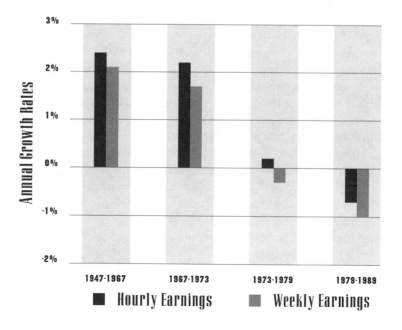

SOURCE: Lawrence Mishel and David M. Frankel, *The State of Working America 1990-91* (Armonk, NY: M.E. Sharpe Inc., 1991), p. 74.

ers in either country. Drawn by cheap labor, alluring investment and tariff policies, and lax regulations regarding community, worker, and environmental protection, many U.S. corporations terminated or scaled down operations in the United States and set up shop south of the border.

The maquiladoras were an outgrowth of a global trend toward production sharing that began in the late 1950s. Once-domestic corporations reorganized to become transnational in scope and began shipping some parts of production offshore to low-wage sites in places like Asia. Facilitated by U.S. tariff laws that had been on the books since the 1930s, U.S. TNCs shifted certain labor-intensive operations abroad and then brought the goods back to the United States for final assembly and sale. According to the terms of the U.S. tariff regulations, when the products reentered the United States, duties were levied only on the value added by non-U.S. labor and by the components and other materials made outside the United States. The TNCs could thus benefit from cheap foreign labor available abroad and not have their payroll savings taxed when the products returned to the U.S. market. When Mexico set up its Border Industrialization Program (BIP) in 1965, it was only one of many developing countries that hoped to capture some of this investment and the job opportunities it promised.

Designed to boost employment in the border region, the BIP was the Mexican government's first major departure from its post-revolutionary strategy of restricting foreign investment and reducing dependence on the international economy. This program waives a number of foreign-investment restrictions and import rules for export-oriented assembly plants. Plants set up under this program, called maquiladoras, may be 100-percent foreign-owned.[24] Along with allowing full foreign ownership, the most attractive aspect of the Border Industrialization Program for foreign manufacturers is the exemption from duties of all imported inputs—materials, components, machinery, and tools. The only stipulation is that the finished product and waste byproducts be shipped out of Mexico at the end of the production process.

The maquila program is an exemplar of production sharing. It usually works this way: A U.S. corporation leases land along the border in Mexico and sets up a wholly owned subsidiary to produce, for example, self-propelled golf carts. The corporation and its U.S. suppliers send components like leather, electric motors, and rubber wheels to the maquila. In addition, suppliers in other locations abroad may also provide components to the Mexican plant. A plant in Singapore, for instance, may provide computer chips for the golf carts. Employees at the maquila assemble the parts into the finished product, package them in Mexican-made foam and cardboard, and ship them to the parent company's warehouse in another border location, where they are stamped "Made in America."[25] The maquila pays no Mexican duties on any of the imported parts, and the parent corporation pays U.S. duties only on the value of the Singaporean computer chips, the Mexican packaging, and the value of the Mexican labor.

The open trade and investment rules characterizing the maquila program encouraged many U.S. corporations to relocate part or all of their production in Mexico. One of the first companies to shift work to Mexico was Fairchild Electronics, which opened a maquiladora in Tijuana in 1966 to take over component assembly previously performed in California. Sears, Roebuck & Co. gave a boost to the program by pressuring its suppliers to shift some or all of their work to Mexico. Sears wanted to trim suppliers' costs but keep the "Made in America" label on its products.[26] Dozens of apparel and appliance manufacturers took the huge retailer's advice. Other Fortune 500 companies followed slowly but surely, along with hundreds of smaller firms. By the mid-1970s, U.S. giants such as Zenith, General Motors, General Electric, Westinghouse, Parker-Hannifin, DuPont, ITT, Quaker Oats, Honeywell, Burroughs, and Motorola had joined companies like RCA and Fairchild in establishing maquiladoras.

Not all new maquiladoras were runaways. In a few cases, old product lines using proven technology were sent to Mexico, to be replaced in this country by newer, top-of-the-line goods, with no loss of U.S. jobs. In other situations, maquiladoras replaced facilities elsewhere—usually in east Asia. But in hundreds and hundreds of cases, the new Mexican assembly plants were tied to corporate decisions to replace higher-wage U.S. production, either directly or through contract bidding in which low-cost maquiladoras won out over their U.S. competitors.

Economic changes and aggressive promotion prompted rapid growth in the maquiladora program. In 1968, 112 Mexican maquiladoras assembled or processed approximately $40 million worth of U.S. inputs for duty-free reexport to the United States.[27] This represented less than 15 percent of the total value of goods the United States imported duty-free that year under the special tariff provisions governing these transactions.[28] By 1977, however, Mexico had eaten into the market share of export-processing zones in east Asia and the Caribbean. That year there were 443 maquiladoras, and the duty-free portion of their exports to the United States totaled $631.1 million—32 percent of the global total. Another nine years later, in 1986, the number of maquiladoras had doubled to 890 and the value of U.S. components they imported, processed, and exported had more than quintupled to $3.4 billion. By 1986 Mexico was processing as many U.S. inputs for duty-free export to the United States as all other countries combined, which continues to be the case today (see Table 1.2). Moving into the 1990s, the sector was still growing. By 1992, the number of maquiladoras had passed 2,000.

The U.S. tariff exemption for offshore assembly of U.S. components encouraged the growing exodus of manufacturing to Mexico, and it is likely that Mexico's weak and laxly enforced environmental and labor standards also played a role.[29] But by far the most important factor in the choice of Mexico as an export-processing site was—and is—the low wages paid to Mexican workers. This fact was made clear by the rapid expansion of maquiladoras after Mexico's minimum wage fell from a high of $1.53 per hour in 1982 to $0.68 per hour in 1983, and then to a range around $0.50 per hour from 1986 through 1990[30] (see Figure 1.6). Whereas in 1981 Mexican workers were paid more in dollar terms than those in South Korea, Taiwan,

TABLE 1.2 ■ U.S. PRODUCTION SHARING
(in millions of $U.S.)

	1975	1983	1991
Total U.S. imports under 806/807	$5,162.4	$21,575.9	$57,527.0
U.S. imports from Mexico under 806/807	1,019.8	3,716.9	14,335.8
Duty-free portion of U.S. imports under 806/807	1,265.9	5,386.6	14,517.2
Duty-free portion of U.S. imports from Mexico under 806/807	552.4	1,968.7	7,254.9

SOURCES: Figures provided by the U.S. Department of Commerce and the U.S. International Trade Commission, *Imports under Items 806.30 and 807.00 of the TSUS* (Washington, DC: U.S. International Trade Commission, various years).

Hong Kong, and Singapore, by 1983 their wage and benefits package had moved into last place among the five countries.[31]

Aware of the importance of wages to investment decisions, the Mexican government has engineered a steady decline in the cost of

FIGURE 1.6 ■ **GROWTH OF MAQUILADORAS AND AVERAGE HOURLY LABOR COST IN MEXICO, 1980–1992**

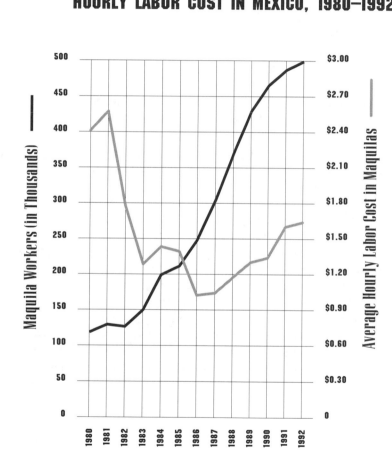

SOURCES: Figures for maquila workers are from *Estadística de las Industria Maquiladora de Exportación 1979-1989*, Instituto Nacional de Estadística, Geografía e Informatica; American Chamber of Commerce, *Maquiladora Newsletter*, Nov. 1990; *Agence France-Presse*, Jan. 1, 1992; *El Universal*, Aug. 19, 1992. Figures for average hourly Mexican labor costs are from the U.S. Department of Labor and the U.S. Bureau of Labor Statistics.

labor by allowing peso devaluations and consumer inflation to greatly exceed increases in the minimum wage. Since 1987 the government has institutionalized the downward wage pressure by concluding a series of economic "pacts" spelling out maximum wage hikes, among other things. From 1982 to 1991 the purchasing power of Mexico's minimum wage declined by 66 percent. In 1992 a minimum-wage worker earned less than $30 per week.

While labor costs plunged, the productivity and technological sophistication of maquiladoras and other export-oriented manufacturing plants climbed, providing added enticements for U.S. runaways. Such plants were no longer limited to labor-intensive industries such as apparel, leather goods, and manual assembly of toys, switches, and other electrical components. Automatic insertion machines and surface-mount technology were added to circuit board assembly lines, clean rooms to the semiconductor industry, and robots to metal-machining processes. Value added per employee—one indication of the technological level of a process—increased from $5,780 in 1983 to $7,794 in 1989.[32] As dozens of state-of-the-art Mexican facilities demonstrate, Mexican workers are quite capable of turning out high-quality, high-technology products—at only a fraction of the costs of similar labor in the United States.

In the United States, the maquiladoras have fueled concerns about deindustrialization and the downward pull on standards for labor, environmental safeguards, and community health and safety protections. Mounting evidence of high-technology maquila production has deepened the gloom by threatening high-paid, skilled workers as well as those who have been competing with low-cost imports for decades. These concerns have been heightened by the possibility of a North American free trade accord. By institutionalizing rules for North American trade and investment that further enhance capital mobility, the free trade agreement could stimulate runaways to Mexico and undermine efforts to make corporations accountable to their workers and communities.

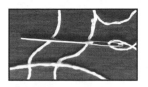

Jobs and Factories on the Move

FOR THE MOST PART, GLOBALIZATION is a gradual process, barely perceptible to most of us. Its march is tracked by esoteric statistics and trends such as the percentage of world trade conducted between affiliates of the same corporation, the number of markets served by an average production facility, and the shifting organization of corporate management structures. Changes in these areas clearly affect our economy, but they rarely attract public attention: a lost contract here, declining market share there, deferred maintenance elsewhere.

Runaway plants, on the other hand, provide dramatic and devastating evidence that the process of globalization is under way. From one week to the next a functioning factory providing a livelihood for dozens or hundreds of residents and contributing taxes to the local government becomes an empty shell with a vacant parking lot patrolled by a handful of security guards. Machinery and leftover inventory are crated away, accompanied by a few employees retained on the payroll to train their Mexican replacements in operations and maintenance.

Runaways do not always follow this stark scenario. Sometimes only a portion of a plant's production will be shifted, or the facility will continue to serve as a distribution center, for example. In all cases, however, runaway jobs represent the most direct consequence of globalization. The nationality of a work force is changed but everything else—machinery, distribution networks, consumers, and the sources of capital—remains the same.

At least 100,000 people in at least 250 work sites in the United States saw their jobs shipped to Mexico in just this way during the last dozen years. These figures do not include job losses due to layoffs in supplier industries or local businesses dependent on the payrolls of runaway plants. In Appendix A we list the cases we have documented of jobs exported by U.S. corporations. Although there are many cases that escaped our attention, and although runaways represent only the most visible effect of globalization, our study sheds light on the forces at work in the U.S. economy and the challenges they pose to workers and civic leaders. Examining the reasons jobs are sent to Mexico adds concrete evidence to common-sense notions of the threats represented by unbridled competition for profits among companies, and for jobs and investment among countries.

This chapter combines a discussion of the primary factors behind the export of jobs with case studies of runaway plants that illustrate each point. Two factors stand out as explanations for runaways: large wage differentials accompanied by similar productivity levels, and the availability in many developing countries of a young work force unwilling or unable to challenge management's control over the work process. One or both of these factors is usually the driving force behind a company's decision to relocate work to Mexico and other low-wage countries. Another factor is less important in general but potentially decisive in specific industries: Mexico's relatively lax enforcement of its regulations covering occupational safety and environmental protection.

The Low-Wage Solution

Most runaway jobs involve labor-intensive activities such as manually inserting capacitors or transistors into printed circuit boards, bundling wires for electric appliances or cars, sewing garments, assembling toys, processing coupons, or assembling switches, thermostats, or other electric components. Of the jobs we have documented as running away to Mexico, at least 75 percent are in activities that are predominantly labor-intensive, and approxi-mately 15 percent are clearly not labor-intensive[1] (see Table 2.1). Wages (and benefits, if any are provided) represent a large portion of the total operating costs of the plants where labor-intensive tasks are performed, making the potential savings from moving to low-wage countries very attractive.

Another reason that labor-intensive work is especially vulnerable to relocation abroad is that industrial engineers can often break down such work into many small operations that require only a few hours or days of training. A minute division of labor helps runaway firms reduce the complications stemming from replacing an experi-enced work force with a new one. Foster Grant, for example, em-ployed 340 people until 1986 in Leominster, Massachusetts, to assemble its sunglasses. After shifting the work to two maquiladoras in Nogales, Sonora, managers encountered an astronomical em-ployee turnover rate of 400 percent per year. If weeks of training had been required for each new employee, any cost savings from the relocation would have been wiped out. But Foster Grant's assembly process is divided into such tiny operations that many workers re-peat their operations every five seconds, reducing training needs to a bare minimum.[2]

A number of entrepreneurs have made an extremely lucrative business out of educating manufacturing executives about the sav-ings they can enjoy by replacing their U.S. workers with Mexicans. In brochures, videos, seminars, and personal visits, companies like Assemble in Mexico, Cal Pacifico, IMEC, and Inter-American Hold-ings claim they can save the right kind of firm between $10,000 and $22,000 per year per job transferred to Mexico. Many so-called eco-nomic development organizations on the U.S. side of the Mexican border have mounted their own campaigns to promote runaways in the hopes of attracting managerial, technical, and advanced manu-facturing employment to their cities.

The focus on cutting labor costs in individual companies has been accompanied by an oft-repeated assertion that U.S. workers are overpaid. Then-Federal Reserve Board Chairman Paul Volcker told a congressional committee in 1979 that "there's no way you can avoid a decline in the standard of living for the average American." Motorola chief executive officer Robert W. Galvin explained on the eve of relocating half of his firm's manufacturing jobs to Asia that "American labor can't compete" at current wages. In 1987 General Electric's chief economist added moral teaching to economic disci-

TABLE 2.1 ■ WORK-SITE JOB LOSSES BY INDUSTRY

INDUSTRY	NUMBER OF RUNAWAYS	NUMBER OF JOBS LOST	PREDOMINANTLY LABOR-INTENSIVE
Apparel & Related Products			
Apparel	21	8,000	Yes
Automotive seat belts & covers	4	2,700	Yes
Medical garments	1	200	Yes
Automotive			
Assembly	2	3,700	
Engines	1	500	
Glass	1	4,300	
Parts (nonapparel, nonelectrical)	13	5,400	
Chemical (batteries)	3	600	
Consumer Durables			
Small appliances	7	2,000	Yes
Televisions & TV parts	10	11,700	Yes
White goods (refrigerators, ranges, etc.)	6	1,600	
Data Processing	2	200	Yes
Electrical			
Auto (lights, signals, switches)	7	1,800	Yes
Components (switches, transformers, etc.)	34	6,300	Yes
Electromechanical (thermostats)	5	1,200	Yes
Lighting products	8	700	Yes
Motors	9	4,200	Yes
Electronics			
Auto (car radios, microelectronics)	4	6,300	Yes
Circuit board assembly	2	300	Yes
Components (resistors, ballasts, etc.)	19	9,600	Yes
Semiconductors	4	1,600	
Other	2	300	Yes

INDUSTRY	NUMBER OF RUNAWAYS	NUMBER OF JOBS LOST	PREDOMINANTLY LABOR-INTENSIVE
Food Processing	2	800	Yes
Footwear	4	800	Yes
Furniture	11	4,000	Yes
Medical Products	9	1,100	
Metalworking (casting, welding, machining, plating & assembly)			
Heavy equipment	3	700	
Combustion motors, not automotive	2	500	
Machine tools	2	n/a	
Other products	11	2,600	
Office Equipment	3	1,200	
Plastics Manufacturing	8	1,600	
Repair Services	1	200	Yes
Wire Harnesses			
Automotive	12	4,400	Yes
Other Uses	10	1,400	Yes
Wood Products	1	100	
Miscellaneous Assembly	4	1,800	Yes
Miscellaneous Manufacturing	10	1,900	
TOTAL	258	97,000	

pline, asking "what in the Bible says [Americans] should have a better living standard than others?" And Dr. Lawrence Krause, a senior advisor to the Pacific Economic Cooperation Council, defended the downward pressure on blue-collar wages resulting from free trade, telling a group of congressional aides that "there is no reason in the world that high-school graduates should be making $40,000 a year" in manufacturing jobs.[3]

Few blue-collar workers make that kind of money, and those that do are generally skilled technicians with significant post-high-school training. Outside the abstract world of free-market economists, the claim that overpaid U.S. workers are to blame for runaway plants is not credible. The average wage for a manufacturing production worker in 1991 was $12.16 per hour, or about $25,000 per year. Eleven countries, including Germany and Japan, paid their workers more that year.[4] In addition, the labor-intensive activities that are most likely to relocate to a low-wage country are among the lowest-paid in U.S. industry, even when they are unionized. As often as not, runaway employers are replacing $6.00- to $9.00-per-hour labor with $1.00- to $2.00-per-hour labor.

The only standard by which U.S. blue-collar wages can be judged to be excessive is that of developing-country workers, who do not earn enough to pay for decent housing, much less to save for their families' futures. Nevertheless this is the standard to which increasing numbers of workers in industrialized countries are being held. In 1987 a Goodyear Tire & Rubber executive acknowledged as much, telling the *New York Times* that "until we get real wage levels down much closer to those of the Brazils and Koreas, we cannot pass along productivity gains to wages and still be competitive."[5]

The runaway plant phenomenon is a key component in the process by which U.S. blue-collar wages are inching downward to meet those of their developing-country counterparts. In a direct way, the loss of jobs when plants leave town will tend to lower wages. But the indirect effect of runaways is even greater. Evidence that production can be shifted to Mexico or other low-wage countries gives employers a big stick in contract negotiations with workers.

In the mid-1980s General Motors' Packard Electric Division told its union local in Cleveland, Ohio, that workers would have to accept a 62-percent pay cut for new hires or their jobs would go to Mexico. Packard had no trouble backing up the threat, since GM already employed tens of thousands of workers in Mexico at $1.00 per hour and less. When negotiations ended, the union had a small victory:

The new-hire pay scale was cut by only 43 percent. In Centralia, Ontario, Fleck Manufacturing carried out a similar threat: Only hours after its work force went on strike in response to demands for wage concessions, the plant closed down and moved to Ciudad Juárez, Mexico. From the NASSCO shipyard in San Diego to Ertl's toy factory in Iowa to the Gould electronic components plant in Newburyport, Massachusetts, corporate executives have explicitly used the threat of running away to extract wage and benefits concessions from workers.

CASE STUDY | Living and Dying by the Invisible Hand

The city of Knoxville straddles the Tennessee River near its source in the ancient, green hills of the Appalachian Mountains. Both the river and the highways around Knoxville follow the dictates of geography, paralleling the worn rock ridges from northeast to southwest.

Knoxville's relatively brief industrial history has followed a similar path. Textile mills moved from New England to Tennessee, rapidly bringing the city into the industrial age. By the mid-1960s textiles had become the mainstay of the flourishing local economy, providing work for thousands. But what capital mobility brings, capital mobility can take away. In 1985 Knoxville saw over 200 jobs move on down the road southwest to Mexico. In just a few decades the city had passed through the industrial revolution and moved whole hog into the global economy.

The Jim Robbins Company was a relative latecomer to Knoxville, arriving in 1966.[6] The firm, a seat-belt supplier to Ford Motor Company, had recently received great news: Ford would equip its new cars with belts in the rear seats as well as in the front. Within days company officials had leased a factory and hired workers; within weeks the plant was producing 50,000 seat belts per week.

Robbins added two more plants in quick succession, bringing the firm's local work force to 1,200, supplying 60 percent of Ford's demand and a good chunk of General Motors'. According to local papers the Robbins complex in Knoxville was the largest seat-belt-manufacturing company in the world.

There was little question why Robbins had chosen to expand in Knoxville rather than in its home state of Michigan. Speaking at the dedication of its third Knoxville plant in late 1967, a company executive extolled the town's residents and their work ethic. "The work force has a progressive attitude and a desire to work which is essential for industrial growth. . . . They're good workers and they're intelligent too. Your labor force here trains very quickly." Not much hidden by this rhetoric was the fact that Knoxville workers would perform their jobs for just over half what similar workers in Detroit demanded: $2.58 per hour versus $5.04.

With a skilled work force and an existing industrial base came a union, however. The Amalgamated Clothing and Textile Workers Union succeeded in organizing Robbins in 1967. The union's success may have been behind a warning delivered by the firm's president that year. "The future of our expansion in Knoxville," he announced, "depends on the business atmosphere."

Apparently the business atmosphere was favorable through the 1970s. By 1979 the company—now owned by Allied Chemical, an industrial giant—was one of the largest employers in Knoxville, with nearly 3,000 employees. But over the next few years the company laid off about 2,500 workers.

In part the layoffs were due to the recession that gripped the country at that time. But another portion of the job loss resulted from the firm's decision to shift investment from Knoxville to Greenville, Alabama. From 1980 to 1985 employment at the firm's Greenville plant rose from 300 to 960. In a near-replay of the Knoxville plant's dedication, company officials proclaimed that Greenville offered a "large and motivated work force, most easily trainable and many already seasoned in industrial sewing, thanks· to the area's history of textile and carpet production." In addition, a company executive extolled the "upbeat, cooperative, ready-to-serve attitude of local officials and business leaders."

Once again, there was a clear subtext to the company's statements. Greenville was more rural than Knoxville, and less hospitable to union organizing. Equally important, manufacturing wages there were roughly 60 percent of those being paid in Knoxville. These factors allowed Allied to demand wage and work-rule concessions from the Tennessee employees. After 1980, "the company increasingly used job blackmail against us, playing the Knoxville workers off against the Alabama employees," complained a union official.

Having lost over 2,000 jobs, the union capitulated in 1982, accepting pay cuts and new, "flexible" job descriptions that gave supervisors more leeway in assigning jobs to workers. A few jobs returned from Alabama, as the company had offered, but not for long. In August 1985 the seat-belt operation—now known as the Bendix Safety Restraints division of the Allied-Signal Corp.—dumped more than 200 people and shifted their jobs to the small town of Agua Prieta, Mexico. In 1987 the company also transferred a number of production lines from Alabama to Agua Prieta, and in 1988 it announced further job transfers out of Knoxville.

Given the firm's record, there is no telling how long it will maintain production in Agua Prieta, but the location would seem to meet the company's wage and worker-relations goals. Like the half-million Mexican workers employed by export-oriented industrial or service companies all along the border, the new Bendix employees in Agua Prieta receive far less than even the low wages paid to Knoxville workers. Instead of paying an average of $5.76 for an hour of an employee's time, Bendix is now spending under a dollar. And in Agua Prieta the threat of a hostile union winning the right to represent the work force is remote. The local union bosses act as an arm of the Mexican government, which is doing all it can to encourage foreign investors.

Beyond Wage Competition ... to Union Busting

If wages were all-important in deciding where businesses locate, countries like Haiti, Bolivia, and China would claim a larger share of runaway manufacturing. Other costs also influence executives' decisions about where to move. These include getting supplies to a plant and getting goods to market, coping with unreliable communications systems, training the work force, carrying increased inventory to guard against supply disruptions, and learning to operate in a place with different laws, customs, and language. Political risk—the likelihood of social upheaval or expropriation of investments, for example—is another important consideration.

These factors tend to encourage manufacturers to locate operations in their home countries or in established industrial areas. But in many cases the extent to which they constitute obstacles to investing abroad diminishes each year. Competition among developing countries for foreign investment drives their governments to become ever more responsive to the needs of international investors. Governments are cutting red tape, improving infrastructure, subsidizing worker training, controlling labor activism, and doing what they can to ensure policy stability.

Complementing the efforts of these governments are private relocation consultants located in both high-wage and low-wage countries. For a hefty fee, firms like P.H.H. Fantus of Chicago will use their knowledge of different legal systems and their carefully cultivated access to government and industry leaders to help a runaway firm set up shop quickly and avoid possible pitfalls.

Possibly the most important pitfall firms wish to avoid is that of hiring what turns out to be an assertive and organized work force. The significance of this issue is evident in corporate relocation decisions within the United States, since labor law and the strength of unions vary greatly from state to state. In the late 1970s a Fantus employee told the head of New Mexico's industrial development commission that half of its corporate clients would not even consider locating a plant in a state that did not have a so-called "right-to-work" law on the books.[7] (These laws undercut union organizing by prohibiting mandatory union dues even at plants where a majority of workers vote in favor of unionization.) A huge, joint MIT-Harvard study in 1980 found that "a new work force that is nearly impossible to organize is perhaps the most prized side benefit of a new plant site, and it is the controlling consideration for many companies." The study's survey of new or relocated plants found that by far the most important factor in choosing a region or state was the presence of a "favorable labor climate." Low labor rates, in contrast, ranked fifth.[8]

The same concern applies to international relocation. A government's ability to ensure a stable, cooperative work force over the long term is one of the chief reasons some low-wage countries have succeeded in attracting scores of export-oriented companies while other countries lag behind.

Mexico is well aware of this fact. The country's maquiladora sector has been characterized by very low rates of unionization since its inception. The government and—with a very few exceptions—the unions themselves have seen to it that independent, aggressive forms of labor activism among maquiladora workers are soundly quashed.[9]

Since at least the early 1980s the Mexican government has expanded its efforts to rein in labor activism beyond the maquiladoras in order to establish favorable conditions for foreign investment throughout the economy. The strong legal protections for workers and unions that were established after the Mexican revolution have always doubled as tools of political control.[10] Union leaders and politicians consistently traded workers' support of the party and the system for government protection and highly selective punishment of union corruption. The trade-off, however, has become increasingly one-sided over the last decade. The ruling party has used its tremendous leverage over union leaders to persuade them to accept large cuts in real wages as well as labor contracts that eliminate traditional protections from management abuses, including well defined job descriptions, shop floor representation, and seniority-based promotion and job-security systems.

Protections such as these rank very high on the list of reasons that corporate managers attempt to weaken or avoid unions. In part this is due to traditional management training and habits, which place great importance on retaining control of the workplace. But it is also due to recent trends in technology, marketing, and the organization of work that stress maximizing flexibility in order to respond quickly to changing market demands. Corporate negotiators have often threatened to shift jobs to Mexico during contract talks to extract concessions not in wage and benefits packages, but in systems of job classifications, work rules, or restrictions on hiring and firing workers.

The latter issue was what executives at Iowa-based Ertl focused on in 1985 when they threatened to shift work to an existing plant in Tijuana. "They told us that our jobs would be moving unless we gave them the right to hire more temporary employees. We had no choice but to go along," said a local UAW official.[11]

CASE STUDY | "Flexibility is Job One"

Mexico's enforced labor docility helped draw the attention of executives at Ford Motor Company in the mid-1980s. Ford was just recovering from massive financial losses, and the entire U.S. auto industry had been withering since the 1970s from a combination of low-price, high-quality Japanese imports, rising gasoline prices, and falling market demand. No longer able to rake in oligopolistic profits from both domestic and foreign markets, the "Big Three" U.S. automakers[12] turned to cutting costs and regaining managerial control over the organization of work. Both goals required weakening the United Automobile Workers union (UAW).

Ford and General Motors launched a "southern strategy," building new assembly and parts facilities well away from the UAW's traditional base. Until the 1970s, nine out of ten North American auto workers lived within the triangle formed by Cincinnati, Milwaukee, and Toronto.[13] By 1990 a map of automotive employment gave the impression that a tap had been opened at the Cincinnati point of the triangle, causing jobs to flow in a stream through Kentucky and Tennessee, then spread out in the southern United States and along the Texas-Mexico border.

The search for cheaper labor was by no means the only reason for moving out of the upper Midwest. In some parts of the car-making process—casting, machining, and stamping, for example—machine up-time is more important than labor costs, which is why car companies had been willing to pay premium wages in the past. In addition, Japan's competitive challenge was based not only on the low price of its cars but also on rapid upgrades in performance, features, and styles. Keeping pace with these frequent upgrades required new applications of technology and new ways of organizing work. Executives who had long disliked the narrow job classifications negotiated by unions now pushed hard to broaden job descriptions and to give supervisors the flexibility to reassign workers among job stations at will.

Ford took the lead in implementing more flexible forms of work organization in the United States after obtaining significant work-rule concessions from the UAW. In the mid-1980s, as the company considered where to locate production of its next generation of small cars, Ford decided to go one step further. Although it had laid off tens of thousands of Michigan workers in the previous few years, the company did not locate the new facility in that state. Instead it extended the southern strategy into Mexico in pursuit of nearly complete flexibility. Boldly investing $500 million where no auto company had gone before, the company set up a modern, automated stamping and assembly complex in Hermosillo, 160 miles south of the Arizona border.[14]

The labor force in Hermosillo had never worked in the automobile industry, presenting a challenge for trainers but a golden opportunity for supervisors. Careful screening, the strong attraction of roughly $1.10 per hour in starting wages, and the Mexican union's cooperative attitude[15] gave Ford the contract its managers had dreamed about: All workers would be classified simply as technicians and seniority did not have to be considered in making promotions. In many areas of the plant there would not even be a distinction between skilled maintenance workers and assemblers.

Taking full advantage of this flexibility, Ford has organized production around teams of workers. Modeled on the system used in Japan by Mazda—and in some ways surpassing that system—the Hermosillo plant has been successful beyond the expectations of its planners. Within three years the plant was producing Ford's top-quality car, the Mercury Tracer, which virtually tied the Honda Civic as the highest-quality subcompact sold in the United States in the 1989 model year. Based on this performance Ford invested $300 million more in the plant in the early 1990s, significantly increasing the complexity of the operation by adding two versions of its best-selling Escort to the production lines.

The Escort lines were moved to Mexico from Edison, New Jersey. Although no one was laid off in Edison because Ford assigned a different vehicle to the plant, Ford's investment in Mexico represented capital it was not investing in the United States. The plant's success also served to undermine activists within the UAW who opposed the union's cooperation with the "flexibilization" of work rules in Ford's remaining U.S. plants.

Of great importance to unionists seeking to establish cross-border ties, Ford's move to Hermosillo actually weakened the Mexican union that represents Ford workers in that country. The company was able to hold Hermosillo's high productivity and favorable contract terms over the heads of workers at its existing plant in Cuautitlán, just north of the capital city. Thanks to the Mexican government's earlier support of industrial unions, workers in Cuautitlán received twice the pay of their counterparts in Hermosillo, and their labor contract established well-defined job classifications. Three years after Hermosillo came on line, however, the Cuautitlán workers buckled under to the company's pressure—augmented by violent, union- and government-abetted repression—and accepted deep wage cuts, the selective firing of activists, and more flexible work rules.

The Lethal Attraction of Lax Regulations

Closely related to the interest in weakening or avoiding unions is the desire by some firms to minimize both worker awareness of and corporate liability for occupational safety and health abuses. Unscrupulous managers have been able to satisfy both objectives in Mexico.

Workers are rarely able to read the English-language warning labels on barrels of chemicals, and they usually lack the education and industrial experience that might lead them to question the safety of their jobs. Even as word spreads of colleagues who have fallen victim to work-related poisoning, the increasing numbers of workers who understand they may be trading their health or their lives for a dollar an hour find they have little recourse. If they speak out they may be summarily fired. If they turn to the courts they will find that the Mexican legal system does not allow individual citizens to sue corporations that violate occupational or environmental laws.[16] Only if the government or a union decides to take up a case can a corporation be sued for violating worker health and safety standards. Such intervention has rarely occurred in the past. Given the combined government-organized labor effort to establish a good business climate for foreign investors, it is unlikely to occur in the foreseeable future.

Some of the most hazardous industrial activities are among the most prominent segments of the maquiladora sector. For example, over 50,000 Mexicans assemble printed circuit boards or their components, an activity that exposes many of them to toxic solvents and solders, some of which are known to cause cancer. The value of furniture production in the maquiladoras—in which workers inhale sawdust, lacquers, and paint fumes—increased nearly seven times from 1982 to 1990. Plants producing plastics, rubber products, or other chemicals multiplied twentyfold in the same period, and the value of their output soared to a whopping 123 times its previous level.[17]

This circumstantial evidence indicates that the attractions of manufacturing in Mexico are enhanced for companies in industries in which workplace hazards are significant. Although it is impossible to assess accurately the importance of weak occupational safety laws and regulation in plant relocation decisions, our research uncovered a number of suggestive cases.

In one, a GTE Corp. subsidiary named Valenite shut down production in Syracuse, New York, Riverside, California, and Ontario, Canada, and moved to Mexicali. Employees in the United States and Canada had complained for years that the cobalt dust they were inhaling caused Hard Metals Disease. Company officials were found to have violated relevant laws or regulations in both countries. After the U.S. and Canadian plants shut down, investigative reporter John

Alpert went to Mexicali, where he filmed poorly ventilated work areas covered with cobalt dust.[18]

A second case began with a multiyear effort by Kast Metals Inc. to prevent Iowa's state occupational safety and health agency from inspecting its facility in Keokuk, Iowa. Five years after winning the court battle, inspectors fined the company $2,000 for "serious violations." Although the fine amounted to a slap on the wrist, the prospect of continued inspections may have played a role in Kast Metals' decision to shut down and move to Ciudad Camargo in the Mexican state of Chihuahua.[19]

In a third example, Schlage Lock, a subsidiary of Ingersoll-Rand, moved one of its manufacturing operations from Rocky Mount, North Carolina, to Tecate, Mexico. Just months before the plant closed in 1988, workers had formed a group called "Schlage Workers for Justice" with the valiant twin objectives of both keeping Schlage open in Rocky Mount and investigating reports by federal authorities and others of toxic chemical emissions. The group's work continued after the plant closed, eventually producing a list of thirty Schlage workers who had died of cancer, possibly the result of handling chemicals. The company denied any connection to the cancer deaths, but did agree to pay the costs of cleaning up its former facility after the U.S. Environmental Protection Agency discovered several hundred barrels of toxic sludge there.[20]

Garment assembly, one of the industries most affected by runaway production, carries high occupational health risks. This is due not to working with hazardous materials but to repetitive motion. When the Levi Strauss company closed one of its plants in Texas in 1990, shifting the work abroad, an estimated 10 percent of the work force was receiving worker's compensation, largely for carpal tunnel syndrome, a common repetitive-motion disorder. According to a company spokesman, the plant had experienced no more injuries than other Levi plants.[21] The problems associated with repetitive and fast-paced jobs may well be even worse in Mexico. According to the Chicago-based National Safe Workplace Institute (NSWI), "Most maquiladora assembly plants have accelerated work processes 25 percent greater than they would be in the United States."[22]

Occupational health problems are by no means limited to factories south of the border, but Mexican workers are even less protected than their U.S. counterparts. "We found that workers are seldom given training, that machinery is not safeguarded, and that instructions on chemical hazards are nearly always written in English," wrote the NSWI. "Work-related injuries and illnesses are typically ignored, and workers who complain are typically discharged."[23] Mexico has made little progress on regulating the levels of toxic gases inside plants or improving other occupational health standards in Mexican factories. Nor does Mexico have an agency equivalent to the U.S. Occupational Safety and Health Administration (OSHA). Predictably, workplace accidents are more common in Mexico. In 1989 there were twenty-six incidents of partial amputations at factories in Nogales alone. Altogether there were 2,000 accidents in Nogales maquiladoras—about three times the rate experienced at comparable factories in the United States.[24]

Unfortunately there is not enough scientific evidence to make any overall conclusions about the severity of occupational health problems inside Mexican industrial facilities. Although anecdotal evidence is deplorably abundant, businesses have fiercely resisted most systematic studies of worker health and safety by denying researchers access both to company records and even to factories themselves.[25]

CASE STUDY | GTE Makes a Run for the Border[26]

The Lenkurt division of GTE Corp. came to Albuquerque, New Mexico, in 1969 from San Carlos, California, in the northern reaches of the Silicon Valley. Fourteen years later, GTE moved over 90 percent of its Albuquerque jobs to Ciudad Juárez. Mexico's low wages clearly played a large role in the company's decision, but thanks to an in-depth study of work conditions at the plant, it is evident that the company sought more than just low wages. Another corporate goal was an environment in which occupational health problems would neither interfere with production nor pose a financial liability.

Certainly this was true when GTE moved to New Mexico from California. Like many firms relocating to the sunbelt, GTE was interested in Albuquerque because of the city's reputation as being relatively free of union activity. According to one New Mexico official familiar with the case, "It wasn't just money [higher union wages]" that GTE wished to avoid, "it was [union] interference in management prerogatives." Another official directly involved in negotiating GTE's move to Albuquerque backed up this assessment. "I think they were having labor problems over in San Carlos," he noted.

GTE's labor "problems" continued in Albuquerque. Just two years after the plant opened, the International Brotherhood of Electrical Workers (IBEW)—which had represented Lenkurt workers in San Carlos—succeeded in convincing a majority of the division's workers to sign union cards. This success came despite a vicious antiunion campaign by the firm that resulted in multiple sanctions by the National Labor Relations Board. When the company finally recognized the union two years after its election victory, the Albuquerque plant joined the tiny minority of U.S. electronics businesses that are unionized.[27]

In retrospect, at least one source of the firm's labor problems, and at least one reason GTE wished to avoid unionization, seems clear. GTE Lenkurt's disregard of the health and safety of its workers was mind-boggling. In Department 320, for example, workers mixed epoxy cement in cone-shaped paper cups or handmade cones of foil, stirring the mixture with pencils or toothpicks. Lenkurt had altered the epoxy formula to greatly speed its setting time by mixing products from Shell and Hysol Corp., against the written warnings of both manufacturers. The chemical mix gave off fumes that caused asthma-like breathing problems, eye damage, and skin sensitization. The chemicals are also suspected carcinogens. There was no special exhaust system for these areas.

In Department 341, circuit boards were "stuffed" with components whose leads were then soldered all at once. According to one worker in the department:

> I've had my hands in freon many, many times. It gives off a white fog and it turns your skin white. I sat with my head over heated freon and solder for hours at a time. A lot of times we'd have freon all over the floor. We had fans about once a week. My throat was irritated constantly, my sinuses were always infected. Beginning in 1978 I had a continuous cold for a year and a half. My doctor sent a note in saying I should stay away from whatever was making me sick, but the company said no restrictions or I'd lose my job, and I couldn't afford to lose the job, so I'd ask my doctor to take the note back.

Such stories were repeated dozens of times, but according to Jack Lacy, the company's safety and loss-control officer, corporate executives consistently decided to ignore complaints.[28] Lacy was able to implement some significant changes, but encountered tremendous resistance to most of his efforts.

The end of Lacy's limited reforms came when GTE's corporate leaders warned all plant safety officers that they would be considered "liabilities" if their health and safety programs were not operating "right"—at lower costs—within eighteen months. According to Lacy, after the warning an executive flew out to investigate Lacy's health-monitoring activities. The gist of what he told Lacy was, "If it ain't broke, don't fix it." He said the company was not going to make any changes on anything unless they got caught by the Occupational Safety and Health Administration (OSHA).[29]

In the mid- to late 1970s, the IBEW filed an increasing number of complaints with OSHA about working conditions at Lenkurt. Although these resulted only in preannounced inspections and very minor fines, the possibility of continued activism and higher health and safety costs may well have led GTE to consider moving its operations for a second time. In any case, the company was obviously leaning in that direction, because it wasted no time in acquiring land and buildings in Mexico after that country drastically devalued its peso. In 1983, the same year that Lacy received his cost-conscious visitor, GTE moved the most menial—and dirty—assembly departments from Albuquerque to Ciudad Juárez, some 250 miles down the Rio Grande.

The next year the firm fired Lacy and a number of others, leaving the entire telephone division with a health and safety staff composed of a single industrial hygienist based in Connecticut. Given the corporation's attitude toward its workers, the logistic and linguistic problems facing the lone health officer in monitoring the Juárez plant, and the probusiness orientation of Mexican unions, it would seem a safe bet that GTE's Mexican employees labored under conditions similar to or even worse than those faced by their New Mexican and Californian predecessors.[30]

"Economics" may well have been the main reason for GTE's move, as the company claimed. But more than wages go into economic calculations. In this case the costs of making modifications to improve the health and safety of workers were clearly of concern to corporate headquarters, and the potential for a large workers' compensation lawsuit may also have been a factor. An Albuquerque lawyer filed such a lawsuit on behalf of GTE workers in 1984. Three years later the company settled the case, offering an estimated $2 million to $3 million in compensation to 115 former employees. At least a dozen workers died—most of various cancers—before the settlement was finalized.

Clearing Out Instead of Cleaning Up

Another form of regulation that some companies hope to avoid in Mexico is environmental protection. As with occupational safety and health issues, it is difficult to determine how important environmental considerations are to executives in deciding where to locate a factory. But common sense and anecdotal evidence again indicate its significance to certain firms or industries.

U.S. firms spend a great deal on controlling pollution—approximately $72.5 billion in 1990, according to the Environmental Protection Agency (EPA). The agency predicted that these costs would rise to roughly $90 billion by the year 2000, before accounting for inflation. Total public- and private-sector pollution control expenditures came to 2.1 percent of total economic output in the United States in 1990, one of the highest levels in the world. And for some industries the cost is much more significant. In 1992 the Chemical Manufacturers Association, for instance, estimated that compliance with environmental regulations would cost $2.7 billion that year, representing 21.5 percent of that industry's capital expenditures.

It is also evident that many firms have skimped on their environmental protection measures in Mexico. According to Mexico's counterpart to the EPA (known as SEDESOL), of the 1,963 maquiladoras operating at the end of 1990, at least 1,035 were significant generators of hazardous wastes. Of these, only 307—fewer than one-third—complied with all Mexican environmental laws. In the same year, the California-Arizona office of the EPA received only eighty-five notifications of hazardous waste shipments from Mexico to the United States—"a small drop in the bucket" compared to the volume that should have been reported under the U.S. Resource Conservation and Recovery Act, an EPA official said.[31] Either waste transporters are reporting shipments *to* but not *from* Mexico, or the wastes are remaining illegally within Mexico.

The latter is more likely the case, as evidenced by the frequent discoveries in Mexico of hazardous wastes that have been dumped or stored improperly. In 1990 the Boston-based National Toxics Campaign Fund sampled wastewater discharges at twenty-three maquiladora sites. Laboratory tests revealed that 75 percent of the sites tested were contaminated with highly toxic wastes. A water sample taken near a General Motors subsidiary showed a concentration of xylene that was 6,300 times the standard for U.S. drinking water. An employee told one of the scientists that the company routinely flushes untreated solvents down the drain.[32]

A study sponsored by the International Labor Organization (ILO) found that the home-based operations of transnational corporations generally had better health and safety performance than those of their foreign branches and subsidiaries, particularly those located in less developed countries such as Mexico.[33] It may well be that although most firms practice a double-standard of weaker environmental protection efforts abroad than at home, they do not move abroad in order to save on pollution abatement costs. Instead, plant managers may merely seize the opportunity to cut costs by, for example, dumping solvents down the drain rather than sealing them in barrels and shipping them to an authorized disposal or recycling center. (Obeying the law in this case can cost between $150 and $1,000 per barrel of waste.) In many cases, however, the relevant decisions are made in the plant design stage, implying that environmental abuse is corporate policy. Such decisions are surprisingly commonplace; for example, few new facilities are designed to treat their own wastewater as would routinely be done in the United States.[34]

Ann Bourland, who promotes the state of Sonora to foreign firms looking for a potential business site, views the double standard as natural. "In order to stay in the United States, a lot of these companies would have to invest in very expensive equipment to treat these chemicals and solvents and wastes," she noted. "I've had a couple of companies come down solely for that reason."[35]

A forerunner of the environmental runaways to which Bourland refers may have been the Sonocal Corp. In 1976 the EPA shut down Sonocal's Naco, Arizona, plant for particulate noncompliance.[36] Instead of meeting EPA's demands, the company decided to ship its equipment a few miles across the border to Naco, Sonora.

A recent study by a New Mexico State University professor found that the rates of growth of nine maquiladora industries over the 1982-1990 period were highly correlated with the pollution abatement costs of those industries in the United States.[37] Dozens of furniture firms have escaped southern California's strict emissions standards by moving to Baja California, and the director of the Pasadena Research Institute predicted in 1991 that over the next five years half of the 125,000 metal-finishing jobs in the area will move to Mexico.[38] And according to a survey by the Colegio de la Frontera Norte in Tijuana, about 10 percent of the maquiladoras surveyed cited environmental regulations as a primary factor in their decision to leave the United States. Another 17 percent considered environmental regulations an important factor.[39]

These findings are controversial, however. Other studies have demonstrated no widespread pollution-driven relocation of U.S. industries except in a few highly toxic industries such as the manufacturing of asbestos or the processing of such metals as copper, zinc, and lead.[40]

CASE STUDY | Furniture Firms Flock South[41]

The latter half of the 1980s were not good to David Finegood. The owner of Finegood Furniture had built a successful business employing 700 people in Los Angeles County in the manufacture of tables and bedroom sets. But the company's prosperity was endangered by public concern over air pollution in the county, and by a state agency that was determined to clean up the area's skies.

In 1988, Finegood's plants were fined almost $18,000 by the South Coast Air Quality Management District (SCAQMD) for excessive emissions of solvents and sawdust. The year before, employees at one plant called firefighters when a steel drum packed with solvent-soaked rags spontaneously burst into flames. In 1989 another drum caught fire as it was being hauled away. The problems that led to these fires still had not been fixed by 1990, according to an inspector, who issued a citation. And in 1990 the SCAQMD levied a $1,000 fine against Finegood because neighbors of one of the plants complained about odors and dust. To top it off, the SCAQMD announced that by 1996 all furniture makers in its area would have to start using water-based wood coatings in order to cut down on emissions of solvents.

The new restriction was the last straw for Finegood. He closed his two plants, laying off 600 workers, and set up shop in a working-class section of Tijuana. No longer must he deal with the constant intrusions of air-quality inspectors, lawyers for aggrieved workers, or the complaints of neighbors of the polluting factory. Ironically, although his plant apparently meets Mexico's environmental standards, it now puts out more pollution than it did in Los Angeles thanks to the longer working hours in Tijuana. Neighbors of Muebles Fino Buenos complain of dizziness, sore throats, nausea, and the smell of solvents all day long. The fine dust of lacquer settles over nearby homes and vehicles.

Dozens of furniture companies in southern California are responding in the same way that Finegood did. At least forty furniture firms in the Los Angeles area have moved or are planning to move to Baja California. Once these firms have decided to escape mounting regulations, the most attractive location is often Mexico. In part, of course, this is due to the low wages and lack of a worker's compensation system in Mexico. (The latter is a significant expense in the furniture industry.) But it is also due to the sense that while other U.S. cities might follow Los Angeles' lead in regulating emissions, Mexico is very unlikely to do so.

Mexico has no established air quality standard to regulate paint and solvent emissions, despite a dramatic improvement in Mexico's environmental regulations since 1988. And as has already been mentioned, worker safety regulations are very poorly enforced. As one factory owner acknowledged, "I can find lots of Mexican workers in the United States. What I can't find here in Tijuana is the government looking over my shoulder."[42]

Is There a Silver Lining?

THIS BOOK PAINTS A GRIM PICTURE OF DEINDUSTRIALI-
zation, job losses, increasing inequality, and
an apparently irreversible severing of the ties that used to link capital and community. But maybe all this change, though painful, is
good for the country in the long run. Maybe instead of worrying
about it and organizing to slow it, labor and community activists
should focus their energy on gaining greater adjustment assistance
for laid off workers—retraining funds and unemployment compensation, for example—and on creating a better business environment to
attract investment.

Many economists, business executives, and elected officials rec-
ommend just such a course of action. This chapter briefly explores
why these free trade supporters believe that concern about runaway
jobs is misplaced, why many of them believe that an industrial ren-
aissance is just beginning in this country, and why they are wrong.

The free-market ideology that dominates U.S. policymaking holds
that economic efficiency is maximized when market forces—supply
and demand—determine prices (including wages) and strategies (including investment decisions). Although all but the most radical
free-market advocates recognize the need for governments to play

some role in the economy, the overriding concern is to minimize government interference with markets.

Supporters of free trade draw on free-market ideology to argue that trade barriers are necessarily bad, since they interfere with the smooth functioning of markets. Removing tariffs, quotas, and other artificial obstacles, they say, would encourage a more efficient allocation of resources and benefit all parties in the same way that each of the states of the United States benefits from free trade with the other states.

To back up their assertion of global benefits, free trade supporters cite what is called the theory of comparative advantage. Introducing the idea in 1817, British economist David Ricardo demonstrated that if England could produce textiles more efficiently than it could produce wine, and if Portugal could produce wine more efficiently than it could cloth, both countries would benefit from trading textiles for wine. In more general terms, Ricardo's models showed that the welfare of all countries would increase if each nation specialized in making those goods that it produces most efficiently (that is, at lowest cost) and then traded freely with other specialized nations.

Ricardo's conclusions look good, at least on paper. Trade is beneficial, economists maintain, because different countries have different proportions of land, skilled workers, unskilled workers, capital, and other resources. A country with a high proportion of workers to land does well by concentrating on manufacturing goods, and trading those goods for food in the international market.

Applied to the countries of North America, the theory of comparative advantage indicates that Mexico should specialize in products that require large amounts of low-skilled labor relative to capital, while Canada and the United States should concentrate on capital-intensive products, and on products that require highly skilled workers.

From this perspective, a corporate decision to relocate production abroad in search of lower wages is natural and even desirable. Canadian and U.S. manufacturers should build labor-intensive plants in Mexico, where low-wage labor will lower production costs and therefore prices. Cheaper goods will save consumers money and will help North American corporations compete with low-wage producers elsewhere. Moreover, the alternative to producing in Mexico may be moving to Asia, in which case fewer supplies would be purchased from the United States.

Consumer savings and higher corporate profits will provide investment capital, free-market reasoning continues. More investment will create new, more productive jobs in Canada and the U.S. to replace the unskilled jobs lost in uncompetitive industries. In addition, the investments in Mexico will provide jobs, stimulating economic growth. The investments will also raise labor productivity in Mexico, which free-market economists assert will eventually raise wages there. Growth and higher wages mean greater demand for imports, most of which will come from Mexico's free trade partners, boosting their economies further.

What's Wrong with this Picture?

The evidence of the last two decades poses a problem for the theory of comparative advantage. Trade has steadily increased as a proportion of the U.S. economy, and low-skilled jobs have been shipped to low-wage countries at a rapid clip, but wages have gone down rather than up and jobs have moved from the manufacturing sector to the service sector rather than from low-skilled activities to high-skilled ones.

In part the inability of the U.S. economy to generate sufficient higher-value, better-paying jobs for displaced workers is due to the fact that many of these positions have also been shipped abroad. Mexico's maquiladoras, for example, are no longer limited to low-technology, labor-intensive industries. The trend toward higher-technology manufacturing in Mexico is even more pronounced among foreign-owned facilities operating outside the maquiladora sector. Examples include the engine, stamping, and assembly plants operated by each of the Big Three U.S. auto makers, Cummins Engine's state-of-the-art factory in San Luis Potosí, and the IBM, Hewlett-Packard, and Unisys computer plants that anchor Mexico's own Silicon Valley in and around Guadalajara. These plants export nearly all of their output, competing very successfully with high-technology counterparts in advanced industrialized nations even while employing low-wage labor.

Although labor costs constitute only a small portion of the operating expenses incurred by advanced manufacturing operations such as these, the total wage savings from locating in Mexico can still be substantial. One in-depth study of Ford Motor Company's $500 million stamping and assembly complex in Hermosillo, Sonora, for example, found that Ford saved roughly $100 million per year in wages and benefits over a comparable plant in Michigan while achieving identical or superior quality and productivity. Executives have been so pleased with performance at Hermosillo and at Ford's modern engine plant in Chihuahua that the company has invested $1 billion in the two facilities since 1990 to add capacity and expand the product mix.[1]

The savings at these and similar plants are dramatic despite the highly automated nature of the work because in the United States these jobs would pay premium wages. They are precisely the kind of skilled, higher-wage jobs that free-market economists argue will replace low-wage work sent abroad.

So what are the flaws in the free traders' models? First of all, they rest on the unrealistic assumptions of free-market theory, most notably that there is no long-term unemployment and that markets are competitive rather than dominated by a handful of large corporations. Second, even if free-market economics worked, the theory of comparative advantage is obsolete. When Ricardo developed the theory, a country's capital and technology were nearly as fixed as its land. But these days both cross national borders at will, and modern corporations can establish operations in almost any part of the world. No longer can a country rely on its capital base and technological lead to give it a trade advantage.

To stand Ricardo's example on its head, British textile manufacturers can now move their mills to Portugal to gain access to a lower-wage work force. The combination of British technology and Portuguese labor would then give Portugal a comparative advantage in textiles, causing a decline in British welfare as the country turned to less efficient wine production.[2] In a world of highly mobile capital, better-paid workers in capital-intensive industries can take little comfort in an open trading system. And in a world that is very far from the fully employed ideal, low-wage workers have little chance of advancing without government intervention in the marketplace.

Will Manufacturing Come Back?

In the song "My Hometown," rock singer Bruce Springsteen describes an increasingly common scene in his native New Jersey and across the rest of the country: "They're closing down the textile mill 'cross the railroad track. Foreman says those jobs are going boys, and they ain't coming back."

But not everyone is as pessimistic as Springsteen. A growing school of economic thought argues that new technologies and new ways of organizing work will reverse the exodus of manufacturing activity from industrialized areas, bringing investment and jobs back to better-educated workers in countries with advanced communications systems, and superior research and development facilities.

The new forms of work generally fall under the heading of "flexible manufacturing," and involve highly adaptable machines run by multiskilled operators. The idea is to integrate marketing, design, engineering, and production so that a firm can produce a wide variety of goods simultaneously and respond quickly to changes in demand. This in turn allows companies to tailor their products to very specific market niches and thus to obtain premium prices.[3]

It may be that in some industries flexible manufacturing strategies will succeed in at least retaining, if not regaining, high-wage production jobs. The apparel, electronics, automotive, and specialty steel industries are commonly mentioned as good candidates for this strategy.[4] With appropriate local and federal government initiatives to strengthen worker organizations and encourage a renewed managerial focus on design and production rather than on finance, flexible manufacturing could lead not only to better wages but also to a greater voice for workers in the management of the companies that employ them.

If left up to the private sector, however, it is much more likely that this new production strategy will mean more of the same for workers: unilateral managerial control over basic decisions such as investment strategy and relocation, tight limits on employee input, and job security only for a select few. The predominant corporate vision of flexible production includes combining multiskilled workers with advanced technology. But far from bringing workers into the decisionmaking process as some academic proponents posit, managers can consolidate their own control over the work process by eliminating union-negotiated work rules and seniority systems and by gaining access to a "contingent" work force that can be hired and fired in step with production needs.[5]

As in Ford Motor Company's modern plant in Hermosillo, the quest for a more flexible work force is not necessarily confined to industrialized countries. The Ford plant features possibly the most complete system of team-based production on the continent. This accomplishment is due not to the advanced skills or education of the workers but rather to management's success in doing away with job classifications as well as its ability to screen workers from a very large pool of applicants.

Similarly, AT&T uses a team approach in its microelectronics operations in Ciudad Juárez. According to that division's president, "The average education level in Mexico is about the ninth grade, but it doesn't take more than that to use new manufacturing techniques."[6]

These examples suggest that relying on new technologies and new ways of organizing work to stem or reverse the flow of manufacturing jobs abroad is a risky strategy at best. Without a change in the relations of power between employers and workers or in the accountability of corporations to communities, neither flexible production nor other innovations will change the forces that have driven firms to export jobs and diminish the control that we as individuals and communities have over our future.

Fighting Back: Progressive Responses to Runaways

RUNAWAYS AND DEINDUSTRIALIZATION are such immense problems that it is natural to react with feelings of dismay and powerlessness to the notion of challenging them. But it is possible to overcome those feelings and seek viable solutions, especially when others of vision and compassion join in the effort. Community and labor activists, economists, and social scientists across the United States and around the world are increasingly working together to hammer out programs for sustainable and equitable development. As a result of their efforts, economic strategies are being devised that are intended to enhance popular control over economic decision-making and that may one day harness the process of globalization to serve the interests of people and the environment, not just corporate freedom.

This chapter will discuss several ways to respond to the problems of runaways and deindustrialization, the challenges of globalization and economic development, and the need to gain a voice in economic decisionmaking for those affected by the decisions. The chapter will review selected local, national, and international initiatives that have proven to be successful in retaining family-wage jobs and in building corporate accountability to workers and their communities. Also explored are initiatives that seem promising but that have not yet been tried, such as a national economic development policy and international trade agreements that defend and boost the prospects of workers and the environment, rather than undermine them.[1]

Resolving problems like runaways and deindustrialization requires action on multiple levels, from the local to the global. In a global economy, decentralized local solutions can be undermined easily by international economic processes. At the same time, however, restricting activism to the global level—to the formulation of trade policy, for instance—may fail to produce competitive industries and democratic economic institutions at the level of the local community. Bridging the two levels, national policies and institutions must support local initiatives, transform economic decisionmaking processes, and bolster sustainable development objectives.

Responses must also serve different functions, ranging from immediate actions with limited impacts to long-term efforts to advance the goals of economic democracy and sustainable development. Some programs, for example, are intended to ease the burden suffered by workers and communities as plants relocate and work forces are cut back. Early-warning legislation and displaced worker adjustment assistance are examples of these types of activities. Other initiatives attempt to exert community control over businesses that might otherwise ignore the impact of their actions on workers and communities. These can include requiring corporations to follow through on obligations like job creation as a quid pro quo for receiving development subsidies and tax abatements. Also important are efforts to stimulate economic development and retain or create decent jobs. Still other strategies are intended to create an institutional framework for a globalized economy based on democratic participation that protects workers, communities, and the environment. Trade and investment policies that incorporate specific commitments to raising wages as well as improving working and living conditions in trading partners are essential tools in this effort.

These responses share a common purpose: to make corporations accountable to the public for their private investment decisions. Whether in the United States, Mexico, or elsewhere in the world, workers and their communities are deeply affected by the choices made by corporations seeking to increase the return on their investments. Devising adequate responses to runaways and deindustrialization means, in part, making sure that the costs and benefits of those decisions will be distributed equitably. It also means making sure that community investments in and contributions to corporations—in terms of labor, community services, infrastructure development, and tax incentives—will be taken into account during decisions about plant location.

These are not the conventional responses to the problems of runaways and deindustrialization. The conventional responses are inward-looking, protectionist, misleading, and ineffective. As with the phenomenon of Japan-bashing, they tend to demonize other countries and foreign workers, and fail to raise an effective critique of corporate power, community weakness, and globalization under the current economic system. "Buy American" campaigns, for example, not only miss the point about how production works on the global assembly line, they also fail to enhance long-term economic prospects for U.S. workers. Buying U.S.-made products may save some jobs for a while, but when imports are cheaper and better made, these campaigns make adversaries of consumers who should be labor's ally in community coalitions aimed at increasing public control over the economic decisions that affect their lives.

Likewise, trade barriers that are erected merely to protect local industries from outside competition carry the danger of sheltering inefficient, wasteful enterprises and will not safeguard jobs over the long term. Tariffs and other trade barriers are often defended as a rational response to the subsidies foreign governments provide to their favored producers. But if such barriers are not conditioned on corporate compliance with minimal standards of social welfare and trade-union rights, they will fail to block the international economy's downward tug on wages, working conditions, environmental protection, and health and safety standards. Instead, problems will simply fester behind a protective wall of denial.

The efforts and anger of labor and community activists should focus on transnational corporations, not on other countries and other workers. Responses to economic problems that result from the way the economy and the globalization process is structured need this sort of perspective in order to be successful. The strategies discussed in the following pages stem from a critique of how the economy runs and who benefits or suffers within it. From that starting point, activists are developing a foundation on which to build an economic system driven by values like democratic participation, sustainability, and equity, not just a myopic quest for profit.

Organizing: The First Priority

The crisis the United States faces is both economic and political. Decisions about issues like plant location, investment, and union-busting are made by corporate leaders, but they occur in an economic and political context shaped by government policies. As a result, both corporate leaders and public authorities must be targets of efforts for change. To wage the battle against runaways and deindustrialization, political power—the power of organized communities and interest groups—must be reclaimed and exercised. Moreover, the effort cannot be confined by national boundaries. With globalization erasing the borders between economies, activists must dismantle the barriers between potential political allies in different countries.

Reordering the economy so that it meets human needs will require effective local, national, and transnational organizations. Such strong, broad-based organizations are necessary not only to gain the person-power needed for carrying out projects and for exerting numerical strength in political contests, but also for achieving a broad range of perspectives in the scope of development plans.[2] Among the types of organizations needed are democratically organized unions, labor-community coalitions, and transnational activist networks. These provide vehicles for mobilizing concerned citizens, forums for democratic decisionmaking, and channels for spreading the benefits of development throughout communities.

Organized labor is a key player in the fight for economic justice. Weaknesses within the U.S. union movement, however, have limited its capacity to advance the interests of its own members, much less of the community at large. Historically the labor movement was rooted both in the workplace and in the community, but after World War II, unions became increasingly isolated from other social movements and more caught up in achieving bread-and-butter objectives and plant-floor protections. The conservative AFL-CIO hierarchy contributed to this isolation and, over time, undermined both activism and the strength of organized labor in the U.S. economy and political system.[3] By engaging with the U.S. government and big business in an implicit pact to accept corporate power in exchange for periodic gains in wages and benefits for union members, organized labor in the United States abandoned militancy for a place at the negotiating table. When negotiations no longer resulted in gains—but often in concessions or even job losses—U.S. unions

FOCUS ON FIRR

The Federation for Industrial Retention and Renewal (FIRR) has been one of the most influential groups seeking solutions to economic decline and responses to the challenges of democratic development. Established in 1988, FIRR is a national coalition of community-based organizations working to preserve basic industry and jobs, and to enhance community and worker participation in economic decisionmaking. FIRR is an outgrowth of the Inter-religious Economic Crisis Organizing Network (IECON), which since 1983 has worked to bring together grassroots organizations concerned with economic dislocation. The thirty-two affiliates of FIRR hail from all regions of the country and include community, labor, and religious organizations representing women, ethnic and racial minorities, and all other sectors of the U.S. working class. The organization offers a forum for discussing organizing experiences and developing strategies. It also provides information, technical assistance, and representation on national policy issues.

FIRR and its affiliates have been at the forefront of efforts to save community jobs and to build a democratic, national industrial policy. They have advocated worker ownership, planned manufacturing districts, and regional industrial planning. At the plant level, they have aggressively used early-warning techniques and legislation like the Worker Adjustment and Retraining Notification (WARN) Act to strengthen labor in the face of corporate decisions to relocate operations. They have also fought against the abuse of tax abatements and other subsidies designed to attract industry to set up shop in local communities.

In the search for fair trade that benefits the workers and communities in all participating countries, FIRR and its affiliates are active in two other networks, the Coalition for Justice in the Maquiladoras (CJM) and the Fair Trade Campaign. Through membership in these organizations, FIRR and its members are involved in struggles to force U.S. corporations abroad to live up to environmental, community, labor, and health and safety requirements. Participating in these forums strengthens FIRR's voice in debates over the design of international trade agreements that promote development for all partners.

The most senior members of the FIRR network include the Calumet Project for Industrial Jobs, Tri-State Conference on Steel, Oakland Plant Closures Project, Midwest Center for Labor Research, Naugatuck Valley Project, Industrial Cooperative Association, Seattle Worker Center, Southerners for Economic Justice, and Minnesota Working Group on Economic Dislocation.

found themselves bereft both of militancy and of a critique of corporate power. Abroad as well, the leadership of the AFL-CIO promoted a form of "business unionism" that protected the expansion of U.S. corporations abroad while undercutting elements in foreign labor movements that sought to control corporations and limit their power in the economic system.[4]

Changes in the U.S. economic structure have also limited labor's power. Forces like deindustrialization and the rise of the service economy have transformed the composition of the country's work force. Such trends have decreased the size of the manufacturing sector—labor's traditional stronghold—and increased the number of workers in the service sector. Women and minority workers make up a large proportion of service employees, but have only recently become targets for union organizing.

The onslaught of wage cuts, plant closures, broken strikes, and layoffs during the 1980s prompted U.S. labor to reexamine its relationship to U.S. communities. Many efforts are now being made to organize new workers, build bridges to other social activists, and mount joint campaigns against shutdowns and in favor of initiatives to improve community living conditions and economic stability.[5] Most of these changes have been spearheaded by local rank-and-file movements, sometimes without the support of labor leaders at the national and international levels who still tend to take a conservative, business-unionism approach to labor-corporate relations. The prospect of NAFTA did awaken the AFL-CIO leadership to the need to arrest potential job loss through community coalitions, but such efforts must expand and become more permanent in order to fight successfully against the long-term negative effects of global economic integration.

Once an effective community-worker coalition is established, the real struggle against closures, runaways, deindustrialization, and corporate abuse can begin. The coalition must first work to organize new members and to build strong bases of support both within the workplace and within the community. Once members have been organized and mobilized, the coalition can join the battle as an educator, an advocate, and a participant.

From the Plant Floor to City Hall

By their nature, plant closings are first and foremost a home-front phenomenon. The first responses to them are therefore home-front solutions designed to save jobs and keep the employer in the community or, failing that, to win the best treatment for displaced workers and the most accountability from the corporation.

Reacting at the level of the shop floor or local community holds pitfalls as well as potential benefits. One danger is that the community-worker coalition will simply be reactive, not proactive. Achieving long-term solutions requires thinking beyond just stopping a plant from moving out of town. It requires broadening democratic participation in economic decisionmaking and developing economic development options that broadly distribute the gains of production. In the short term, these grand objectives may be obscured, but keeping as close as possible to that vision can help save a plant fight-back effort from becoming mired in defeat if the closure cannot be stopped.

Another danger is that activists will fail to transform the struggle from an economic to a political one. The battle against shutdowns, disinvestment, and runaways cannot stay confined inside the corporation. Coalition-building is essential, both to avoid the "special interest" tag that gets pinned on labor during these efforts and to achieve broad representation and input during the formulation of economic alternatives. In addition, political authorities must be mobilized to act on behalf of communities. A strong community-worker coalition can help pressure government leaders to overcome their fears about creating an "unfavorable" business climate and to use their authority to seek and enforce corporate accountability.

With these caveats in mind, there are a multitude of possible responses to runaways and deindustrialization. At the plant level, they include setting up early-warning networks, mounting direct actions like demonstrations and occupations, launching consumer boycotts, negotiating protections as part of collective-bargaining agreements, introducing concession bargaining, converting the plant to produce new products, finding a new buyer, initiating worker-community buyouts, inviting government intervention, encouraging community-based actions to force corporate accountability, and engaging in worker-oriented interventions (such as training programs and other assistance to displaced workers).[6] In addition to these plant-specific approaches, intervention can also be aimed at developing regional economies, promoting the health of industrial sectors important to the area, and diversifying the local economic base.[7]

From this large menu, responses must be chosen based on the particular circumstances at a given plant and its surrounding community. That narrows the potential options considerably. If a business is failing because its managers have run it into the ground or because overwhelming market forces have wiped out its ability to

TOOLBOX 4.2 — KNOWING WHAT TO DO DEPENDS ON KNOWING WHERE YOU STAND

There are many factors to consider when deciding how to respond to a possible plant closing. The Midwest Center for Labor Research, whose *Early Warning Manual Against Plant Closings* is still the best primer on the topic of early warning signs, lists several factors that should be evaluated:

■ **Timing.** How much time is there before a closing is planned? Has the decision to close actually been made, or is it still in the evaluation stage?

■ **Reason for the proposed shutdown.** Are there overwhelming market forces which make the plant impossible to save, or are there problems which can be corrected, management decisions which can be challenged?

■ **Relationship between the work force and the community.** Is the local union organization strong? Does it have links with the community? What other potential allies does it have (churches, central labor bodies, sister unions, sympathetic political leaders, neighborhood groups, university researchers)?

■ **Effect a closing would have on the community.** What will be the lost wages, taxes, effect on suppliers, ripple loss of jobs in that community, cost of extra services to the displaced employees?

■ **Resources that are available.** Does the local union have access to assistance from the international union? Staff time? Research? Funding? Do the community organizations have time to contribute to the plant-closing fight? Will the local or state government assist in assessing the situation by assigning staff to it, or by giving a grant to a research group, development corporation, or university department with expertise?

SOURCE: Excerpted from Greg LeRoy, Dan Swinney, and Elaine Charpentier, *Early Warning Manual Against Plant Closings* (Chicago: Midwest Center for Labor Research, 1988).

compete, then it is a poor candidate for a worker-community buyout. Likewise, a weak union on the defensive against a strong, footloose company will have little chance of getting a collective-bargaining agreement that requires the corporation to bargain over the decision to close the operation. In addition, some unions have become so bureaucratized, unrepresentative, and undemocratic that they may have lost the power or desire to speak authoritatively on behalf of plant employees or to mobilize workers in defense of their own interests.[8] In contrast, with enough early warning, a well-organized union with a coalition of backers in the community may be able to halt a potential shutdown or, if that is not possible, to gain a voice in decisions about who the next owners will be or how workers will be compensated in case of a closing.

Whatever option is chosen, the most important resource is an organization that can rally needed resources through coalition-building. Although plant closures trigger the formation of various ad hoc issue groups, the most useful organization is one that exists long in advance of the crisis, has expertise in economic development issues, and has proven skill in developing and mobilizing coalition resources. Across the United States, such organizations are becoming more numerous. They include government agencies with strong grassroots ties like the Steel Valley Authority, national networks and technical assistance providers like the Federation for Industrial Retention and Renewal and the Midwest Center for Labor Research, and local and regional community development organizations like the Calumet Project for Industrial Jobs.

Organizations like these can quickly respond to prospective shutdowns because they can draw on prior experience. Among other things, they can pull together social-impact studies of the predicted effect of a planned closing on the surrounding community, initiate pre-feasibility studies of the worker-buyout option, hold demonstrations and press conferences, and in general get out the information needed to frame the debate and determine acceptable options. These speedy, informed efforts can begin moving political authorities to act on the issue within a couple of weeks, perhaps spelling the difference between a plant saved and a plant stripped of machinery and staff.

Forewarned is Forearmed

The cornerstone of any effective attempt to halt shutdowns and save jobs is a good early-warning network. The federal government attempted to set a national minimum standard for early warning with the Worker Adjustment and Retraining Notification (WARN) Act, which went into effect in 1989. The law requires companies with 100 or more workers to provide sixty days' notice of a closing or mass layoff, but many corporations simply do not comply with WARN provisions. Moreover, the protections do not apply for closings or layoffs involving fewer employees, so plants sometimes gradually drop employees from the roster, thus making sure the law never kicks in. Businesses that run into "unforeseen circumstances" are also spared from sticking to the law's timeline. Even when the WARN Act does work as intended, sixty days' notice is rarely time enough for workers and their community allies to mount a successful bid to stop the closure or to develop alternatives that might save jobs. In fact, the WARN Act is not designed to be a job retention instrument; it is purely a law to help dislocated workers by giving them an opportunity to prepare for job loss and to access training and other forms of assistance.

Ample early warning, however, gives workers an opportunity to devise bargaining strategies, fight-back tactics, buyout options, or conversion plans, and gives sympathetic community organizations time to mobilize public support behind these efforts. It also allows government agencies a chance to get involved while there is still time to intervene—by invoking the power of eminent domain to seize property in the public interest, for example, or by creating a financing package to pull the business through temporary hard times if that is warranted.[9] Even if government agencies cannot intervene to stop a closing or mass layoff, adequate early warning allows more time to develop assistance and training packages for dislocated workers.

Most of the time, the decision to close a plant is one that is made far in advance of the actual shutdown. A 1987 General Accounting Office report found that 92 percent of closings resulted not from failed businesses, but from disinvestment, restructurings, runaways, and the like. These corporate decisions, according to the GAO, typically require one to three years to implement.[10] As a result, those workers who are trained to notice and respond to the warning signals of an impending closure—things like a change in ownership, disinvestment, mismanagement, and duplicate capacity—are in a better position to devise an appropriate intervention.[11]

To help create and empower early-warning networks, the Midwest Center for Labor Research (MCLR) has developed a training program aimed at all those who have regular access to plant-specific information (see Appendix C). Participants in the trainings learn how to spot the signs of a shutdown in the making, even if a given plant is not in any immediate danger of closing. Trainings are customized according to the needs and wishes of the participants, so although information on shutdown indicators is always offered, the sessions may also include a wide range of other topics.[12] For instance, MCLR staff commonly strategize with participants about methods to enforce the terms of development subsidies, to put public pressure on companies to ensure accountability, and to develop coalitions. The individuals and organizations who commonly attend these sessions include local and state economic-development and job-training staff, unionists, neighborhood organizations, churches and religious groups, and business associations. Together, these concerned parties often become the core of a community-worker coalition that can fight back against a planned closure. Besides helping to save jobs, these efforts—by opening channels of participation to people throughout the community—can also help to bring democracy to at least some aspects of the economic decisionmaking that affects community life.

In the cases of Morse Cutting Tool in New Bedford, Massachusetts, and LaSalle Steel in Hammond, Indiana, community-worker coalitions triggered by the early signals of closings managed to keep the plants open. At Morse Cutting Tool, an aggressive campaign backed by the city government—which threatened to seize the plant through its power of eminent domain—forced the parent company to sell Morse Cutting Tool to a buyer who would develop the plant and preserve jobs.[13] At LaSalle, a strong worker-community response not only kept the plant open, but resulted in a strengthened union and plant expansion.[14]

Ownership Options

Winning a voice in decisions about who will own and run a given company is one strategy that has helped stop plant closures and retain jobs. "Ownership," according to activist Lynn Feekin of the Calumet Project for Industrial Jobs, "is the critical factor in a plant's stability. . . . Any other factor can be dealt with, if an owner is committed to keeping the plant alive and operating in that community."[15] The goal is to influence a change in ownership so that the outcome protects jobs and the community. Sometimes the strategy entails finding another buyer; at other times a worker-community buyout may be possible.

TOOLBOX 4.3

CITY PRIDE: BAKING UP SOME NEW IDEAS IN WORKER OWNERSHIP

When Continental Ralston-Purina announced plans to shut down its Braun Bakery in Pittsburgh in 1989, the decision catalyzed worker and community opposition. The 100-year-old bakery was an institution in Pittsburgh, providing family wages for its employees during a time when plant closures in the area were driving thousands from their jobs. Despite early warning of the potential closure, a regionwide boycott campaign, and demonstrations, the workers failed to keep the bakery open. Not willing to give up, the former employees and their union, the Bakery, Confectionary and Tobacco Workers Union Local 12, devised a plan to finance a brand new bakery to be owned by workers, the community, and private investors. Their "City Pride Bakery" is now operational. Although the worker-ownership component of the operation has fallen through, the proposed ownership structure may work in other communities trying to revitalize their own local industries, if some of the pitfalls faced by City Pride are avoided. Even if the ownership structure does not prove to be viable elsewhere, the model of community organizing demonstrated by the City Pride coalition should serve as a lesson for grassroots activists everywhere.

Opening day at City Pride was the result of a long and dedicated struggle. When it was clear that the Braun Bakery would surely close, a community-worker coalition led by the union and the Steel Valley Authority—a grassroots- and labor-oriented development organization—mobilized to rally the public and local politicians behind the idea of a buyout. At the same time, a project team was selected and, working with the coalition, began the long process of turning that idea into a reality. By September 1991, City Pride had received commitments for more than $8 million from a complex range of funders including private venture-capital groups, management investors, banks, neighborhood groups, employee stocks, state pension funds, government agencies, churches, and private foundations.

Either way, it is often useful for the union to act as a possible buyer when it is clear that the plant will be sold. Even if the union is not certain it actually wants to buy the company, this strategy provides access to inside corporate information on sales, profits, market shares, and equipment inventories. Information like this is useful for guiding worker-community action, whatever course is cho-

The ownership structure chosen by the coalition fell through at the bakery because the worker-community partners could not come up with the equity for the Employee Stock Ownership Plan (ESOP). Moreover, neither private banks nor public sources were willing to capitalize that aspect of the operation. Nevertheless, the tripartite ownership structure might prove a model for other communities if equity for an ESOP were available. The model is:

■ Private Ownership. Bakery managers and private investors were to have majority ownership, at least at the beginning.

■ Worker Ownership. Workers were to own up to 30 percent of the firm, gaining a seat on the board of directors.

■ Community Ownership. Neighborhood groups invested nearly 10 percent in the company, winning them a board member and an observer seat on the board as well as "anchoring" the firm in the community.

Like most attempted worker-community buyouts, the City Pride story has not been an unbroken tale of success. In addition to problems financing the ESOP, the new plant had difficulty financing equipment costs, there were some errors made in plant construction, and the initial operation was top-heavy with management staff. But through the efforts of the worker-community coalition, good jobs were saved in the community, and when these problems began to surface, a new buyer was found who has committed to a five-year contract and a worker participation program. City Pride now serves 110 grocery stores and employs nearly 200 workers from Braun and from the surrounding community.

SOURCES: Tom Croft, "Achieving City Pride," *Labor Research Review*, no. 19 (Fall 1992), and interview with staff at Steel Valley Authority, April 12, 1993.

sen. Acting as a buyer has another value: Buyers who intend to slash wages or employment are often scared off once they see how organized and militant labor is at the plant.[16]

In some cases—as with Morse Cutting Tool—an effective worker-community effort helped to screen out buyers who would likely have decapitalized the operation and eventually closed down the plant. At Morse, in fact, the coalition had to mobilize twice, first during a campaign from 1982-84 to influence the parent company's choice of a buyer and then, when the new owner went bankrupt in 1987, to make sure the plant was sold to another company that agreed to keep the shop running. Efforts like these require workers and their community partners to conduct careful research into the needs of the company and into the backgrounds of potential buyers. Under most circumstances, these actions also require strong community support both to pressure the current owners and to prod local governments to insist that the company consider the social costs of the decision when choosing a buyer.

Worker or worker-community buyouts are other ownership options that can sometimes result in saving jobs. A new enterprise can be organized in different ways, whether as a cooperative, through democratically controlled Employee Stock Ownership Plans (ESOPs), or under some combination of worker, private-sector, and/or community control.

Buyouts like these are undoubtedly the most challenging and ambitious response to runaway and plant-closure problems. There are many serious obstacles that have to be overcome, especially with purchases of very large operations. To carry out a successful buyout, the worker-community buyers must surmount problems of financing, training limitations, lack of management experience, marketing and distribution, scale, and the lack of experience with group decisionmaking processes.[17] During the months preceding a shutdown, moreover, many firms are stripped of their equipment and allowed to fall into disrepair as their owners choose other locations for investment. One of the most serious drawbacks is the hardship suffered by the potential worker-owners because of lost wages and benefits during the lengthy struggle to get the rest of these problems settled.

To top it off, even when a plant has been successfully purchased by a coalition of workers and community groups, it must still compete on the same economic terrain that is so harsh to all other businesses of small and moderate scale. The difficulties of competing in such an environment—especially if the operation is tied into the global market—overwhelm many of these operations, even when a worker-community buyout can be achieved.

Despite all their difficulties, worker-community buyouts can be a useful and successful strategy. When they do work out, they not only save jobs, they also help maintain economic stability in the neighborhood. In addition, if they are carefully structured to allow a strong voice for the community and labor participants, they can add democracy to the workplace and contribute to a bottom-up transformation of the economic system.[18]

These positive outcomes are most likely if the worker-community owners can count on some government support, whether from the local, state, or federal levels. The need for training and technical assistance can sometimes be satisfied through government programs, for example. Likewise, government grants and loan guarantees are frequently used to help finance the purchase and to equip the plant. By creating financing mechanisms, training opportunities, and legal frameworks supporting innovative ownership options, government can help workers and communities help themselves.

Getting government assistance may or may not be easy. If the worker-community-corporate relationship is friendly, then building a useful package of available programs may be no trouble. But in a "fight back," government authorities must confront the possibility of creating what might be perceived as a negative business climate. This is where strategy really counts, according to FIRR activist Jim Benn. Coalition partners must force government to act in favor of the public interest—to use its available powers against the corporation. Achieving this goal often requires concerted, long-term effort.

Getting What We Pay For

Given all the advantages held by corporations in the global economy, city and state governments must do everything they can to hold companies responsible to the communities in which they locate. Unfortunately, pressured by plant closures, unemployment, and sluggish growth, many communities have moved in the opposite direction. Like Mexico, many U.S. state and local governments have minimized controls over corporate behavior in order to attract business. Hoping to encourage companies to create or keep jobs in the area, many communities compete for investment by offering generous tax incentives, low-cost financing, and other inducements. Local and state governments across the country have gotten caught up in "bidding wars" with each other, providing everything from worker-training grants to new or upgraded physical infrastructure (like roads and electric lines). These sweeteners have become common-place in many communities, heaping extra demands on homeown-ers, small businesses, and other local taxpayers who have to pay for the programs. In northwest Indiana, for example, nearly all plant expansions and new plants receive a tax abatement, whether they need it or not.[19]

Why would communities take on these extra burdens? In ex-change for such generous subsidies, companies usually promise to create or maintain a certain number of jobs in the area. Almost all applications for subsidies require the company to indicate how many jobs will be created or retained as a result of the assistance. The problem is that the companies often fail to carry through on their promises, and government authorities have been lax in overseeing and enforcing these agreements.

In an effort to put teeth into subsidy applications and agree-ments, some cities and states are changing their laws and regula-tions regarding subsidies. Three major types of reforms are most common:[20]

■ Clawbacks. These are provisions that are included in the ac-tual subsidy contract. If the recipient company fails to achieve the employment goals stated in the contract, or if it moves the jobs out of the facility during the life of the contract, "clawback" provisions require that the company pay back the subsidy on a proportionate basis or in full. In New Haven, Connecticut, for example, the city government enacted a law to require companies that receive public aid as an incentive to locate there to provide six months' advance notice if the company decides to relocate. The company is also re-quired to pay back loans, grants, and tax breaks in full if it should choose to pull out.[21] An even more ambitious ordinance was passed in Gary, Indiana, after an all-out organizing effort by union and com-munity activists led by the Calumet Project for Industrial Jobs. Among other provisions, the Gary ordinance requires the company to provide detailed financial information during the application proc-ess and to report its past history of receiving subsidies, including the number of jobs promised versus the number created. It also requires the city to deny the abatement if the jobs created pay wages less than the prevailing rate or if the company fails to provide a full health-care package for employees working more than twenty-five hours a week.[22]

■ Jobs Impact Statements. Modeled on environmental impact statements, these provisions require that a comprehensive analysis of the impact on employment be carried out before a project is sub-

TOOLBOX 4.4
THE PROBLEM: COMPETING FOR SURVIVAL

General Motors announced in 1980 that it was preparing to close down permanently its last two production facilities in Detroit, but that it would be willing to build a brand-new Cadillac assembly plant locally if the city were willing to make some concessions to the corporation. Otherwise, the new plant would go to a southern location.

What did GM demand? First, the corporation wanted two-thirds of a square mile of land in the middle of the city. The area it wanted cleared was one of the most integrated in the city (51 percent white [Polish], 49 percent Black) where more than 3,000 people lived—far from being a "blighted area." Second, it wanted the city (at taxpayer expense) to relocate these 3,000 people, tear down and compensate 160 small businesses in the area, knock down a 170-bed hospital, remove three nursing homes, redirect two expressway on-off ramps, move a railroad right-of-way, and do something about the two-acre Jewish cemetery in the middle of the plot. The corporation wanted the city then to clear the land to a depth of ten feet below grade so GM would not have to worry about underground water, sewer, telephone, and gas lines. Finally, if the city agreed to all of this and then gave GM a twelve-year, 50-percent local tax abatement, the corporation would agree to build in Detroit. A conservative estimate of the cost to the city (including state and federal contributions) was $450 million dollars.

What is amazing is that the city council of Detroit, including its progressive and socialist members, voted unanimously to give into GM's outrageous demands. The people were removed by eminent domain; the houses, churches, businesses, nursing homes, and hospital were bulldozed. Ironically, because of the depression in the auto industry, the plant is not occupied. Moreover, even if the plant were to go into full operation, only 6,200 jobs would be created—600 less than the number eliminated by the closing of two other GM facilities in the area.

SOURCE: Excerpted from Barry Bluestone, "Deindustrialization and Unemployment in America," *The Review of Black Political Economy* 17 (Fall 1988).

sidized. The analysis must include information on the number, types, and location of jobs that would be displaced or destroyed by automation, relocation, land development, and other features of the project. In addition, those who are affected by the planned operation are supposed to be notified so that they can comment on the proposal and the subsidy application.

■ Legal Actions. Some communities, fed up with shutdowns that have followed generous subsidy programs, have gone to court with their grievances. The success of this strategy is limited by the widespread acceptance—in the public mind and in the law—of the cor-

TOOLBOX 4.5 A SOLUTION: YPSILANTI TOWNSHIP VS. GENERAL MOTORS

General Motors has made a lot of promises it has not kept. Across the country, the corporation has agreed to create and retain jobs in exchange for concessions from communities, later pulling out when relocation offered lower costs elsewhere. But when corporate leaders decided to close down the plant's Willow Run facility in Ypsilanti, Michigan—despite tax abatement agreements committing GM to maintain operations until the year 2003—the township took the corporation to court. Charging breach of contract, the township is trying to get court authority to force GM to keep its plant open and provide the jobs it promised.

Between the Willow Run facility and another GM plant in the area (Hydra-Matic), GM had been receiving property tax abatements from Ypsilanti since 1975. From 1975 through 1990, tax abatements on investments GM made in the Willow Run and Hydra-Matic plants totaled an incredible $1.3 billion. Each time GM wanted to make substantial changes to the product line at one of the plants, corporate officials would invite township dignitaries to lunch, "educate" them about the need for the new product, convince them of the job-creation value to the community, and request a new subsidy. Each time the township complied.

In the case in question, GM received tax abatements on machinery used to produce the Chevrolet Caprice and station wagons. On the application for the abatements, GM said that the new investment would allow the corporation to provide jobs for some 4,500 employees past the turn of the century. In 1992, however, GM decided to consolidate Caprice production in Arlington, Texas, even though Willow Run was a profitable enterprise. The announcement triggered the Ypsilanti lawsuit.

porate right to make "management" decisions about how many employees to hire, where to locate operations, and whether to stay open or to close.[23] Nonetheless, more and more communities have taken companies to court for abusing subsidies. In Duluth, Minnesota, for example, the city won a lawsuit against a firm that used a $10 million Industrial Development Revenue Bond issued by the city to secure a low-interest loan to buy the Diamond Tool and Horseshoe Company. The purpose of the subsidy had been to allow Diamond Tool—the city's largest factory—to stay open, but the conglomerate that bought the company shifted work out of the area instead.[24] The

So far the case has made it through the Circuit Court level in Michigan. Judge Donald E. Shelton agreed with the township attorney that the concept of "promissory estoppel" could be invoked to require GM to fulfill its side of the bargain. Promissory estoppel, a concept from English common law, holds that if a promise is made and favors are granted in exchange for that promise to the detriment of the party granting the favors, then the party receiving the favors is obligated to fulfill the promise. Shelton's order prohibited GM from transferring the production of the Caprice, and Buick and Cadillac station wagons, from Willow Run to any other facility because the Ypsilanti township had granted tax abatements to GM based on the promise that jobs would be retained in the area.

If Shelton's decision is upheld on appeal, it would be precedent-setting. Most breach-of-contract cases require only a cash settlement. No other community has been able to force a corporation to honor the original terms of the agreement, which, in this case, would mean GM would have to stay in Ypsilanti as long as the specified product lines were viable. In addition, Judge Shelton's decision has already threatened GM's plans to shut down another twenty-three plants and lay off 74,000 workers by 1996.

SOURCES: Warren Brown, "Judge Rules GM Can't Close Michigan Plant," *Washington Post*, Feb. 10, 1993; interview with Staughton Lynd, March 26, 1993; Charter Township of Ypsilanti, County of Washtenaw, and State of Michigan vs. General Motors Corporation, Opinion and Order of the Honorable Donald E. Shelton, Feb. 9, 1993.

city of Duluth won the case in court, but similar efforts—in Norwood, Ohio, for example—have been unsuccessful. At the time of this writing, the Michigan township of Ypsilanti was suing General Motors for breach of contract. If successful, the case would establish a precedent requiring not that the company pay back its subsidies, but that it actually stay in town and provide the jobs it promised.

Building Regional Economies

Fighting runaways and deindustrialization sometimes requires regional and sectoral responses.[25] Choosing either of these options definitely involves government in the solution because of the scale of the projects, the political implications of guided development, and the dollars involved. Activities on this level are one step closer to a national industrial development policy because of the coordination and planning that go into making such responses successful.

Some cities have created Protected (or "Planned") Manufacturing Districts (PMDs), for instance, in order to preserve the industrial character of areas threatened by gentrification and redevelopment by commercial projects. As industrial areas are supplanted by these other development projects, good-paying working-class jobs are usually displaced. PMDs, however, are zoning devices that protect industry by prohibiting rezoning to permit gentrification. Carefully controlled—to protect environmental resources, for example—and when included as a package of initiatives to stimulate viable industries, PMDs can help keep jobs within local communities.

Other efforts are aimed at bolstering specific sectors or networks of industries. Through training programs, joint management-worker problem-solving teams, financing, and other support, these programs can help stabilize and invigorate local businesses. On the other hand, such programs must be carefully structured so as to protect and empower workers and communities, not just strengthen the hand of the corporations that benefit from the assistance.

Regional industrial development plans have been devised for some areas that have suffered acutely from deindustrialization. In Pennsylvania, for example, the Steel Valley Authority (SVA) carries out actions designed to enhance economic development in the Monongahela Valley and Pittsburgh area.[26] Although the SVA is a government agency, it is shaped by the needs and strategies of grassroots organizations active in the area. It has used its authority not only to pursue economic development, but also to protect and preserve working-class communities.

Properly endowed, industrial authorities like SVA can have real muscle in the plant shutdown struggle. SVA, for instance, has the power of eminent domain, can seek injunctions to prevent equipment from being moved out of plants, and can levy taxes to raise funds to seek alternatives to plant closings. Such an agency could be a useful tool for other regions as they work to prevent closings, stimulate development, and enhance grassroots participation in economic decisionmaking.

A National Framework for Development

No matter how successful individual communities or regions are in challenging deindustrialization and plant closures, they cannot win the big struggle by themselves. Institutional changes on the national level are needed to adjust the terms of the corporate-worker relationship. In addition, because many of the factors underlying deindustrialization and runaways result from national and global economic structures, coordinated national policies are required to help shape these structures to minimize negative impacts.

To be most useful, national strategies and initiatives should facilitate community-level initiatives and be designed to protect and advance sustainable development at the grassroots level. Federal programs to provide training, education, and financing can help workers develop competitive skills and obtain the resources they need for buyouts and other ownership innovations. Likewise, proworker federal legislation and regulations governing things like minimum wages, working conditions, strikes, and corporate responsibilities regarding closure decisions could help to redefine the corporate-worker relationship in a democratic direction. In addition, carefully targeted federal financing is needed to repair and rebuild the country's physical infrastructure and to give a boost to worker- and community-friendly industries likely to compete successfully in the global economy.

National initiatives that support job retention strategies undertaken at the local and state levels are essential if the fight against runaways and deindustrialization is to be won.[27] The federal government should toughen the WARN Act by lengthening the warning time and lowering thresholds to trigger the law—requiring a full year's notice for plants with 100 or more employees, for instance. It should also require the company to give employees and communities the first option to buy the plant.[28] In addition, the Department of Labor and Department of Commerce should conduct nationwide trainings on early warning signs and WARN Act provisions. These two government agencies could also disseminate information on ownership options, as well as funding pilot projects and sponsoring conferences designed to share information about the most success-ful community responses to runaways and deindustrialization.

Laws would have to change too, as would federal tax code regu-lations. For example, the regulations on major subsidy programs such as Industrial Revenue Bonds, Economic Development Admini-stration grants, Community Development Block Grants, and Job Training Partnership Act assistance need to be written with real teeth to prohibit their use to subsidize job relocation. Likewise, leg-islation is required forbidding corporations from hiring permanent replacements for their striking workers. Without such protection, workers effectively lose their right to strike and, ultimately, their capacity to use their numbers and the threat of withholding labor as a counterweight to corporate strength during negotiations over wages, benefits, and working conditions. Legislation and administra-tive action designed to make it easier to organize and strike would strengthen labor as it confronts plant closures and seeks alterna-tives to them. Other legislation could require the cooperation of plant managers and/or owners with workers and communities when a shutdown is imminent, especially if there have been tax breaks and other subsidies provided to the corporation.

The federal government should also make a stronger attempt to remedy the shortage of effective worker training and retraining pro-grams. Current programs, mandated by the Trade Readjustment Act and the Economic Dislocation and Worker Adjustment Assistance (ED-WAA) Act, are inadequate to meet the need.[29] These programs need to be strengthened by providing longer training periods, allowing recipi-ents to maintain their unemployment benefits while in training, and— most importantly—by training workers for high-wage jobs, not for service-sector positions and other low-wage occupations.

Finally, a national industrial development fund could be estab-lished to provide capital to help revitalize basic industry and other sectors that can support family-wage jobs. A national strategy to modernize basic industry would serve not only to preserve jobs and communities, but also to provide the means to upgrade our infra-structure and the capacity to meet this country's needs for basic goods (e.g. steel). Additionally, a federal fund is needed to provide extended unemployment benefits required for effective retraining measures, and to provide educational assistance, health insurance, and child care while dislocated workers are in transition to new jobs.

Toward a National Industrial Policy

Properly coordinated, each of these initiatives would be part of a national industrial development strategy. People in the United States often oppose the idea of economic planning because they fear big government and associate such planning with socialism. But economic planning goes on all the time in this country. The problem is that it goes on behind closed doors and is carried out by people who have immense power over the lives and livelihoods of U.S. citizens, but who have not been elected and are not accountable to those whose lives they affect. As the Tri-State Conference on Steel observed:[30]

> The demand for an industrial policy is born from an understanding that the people of the United States have no real voice in shaping their economic destinies. Business decisions that determine the resources and futures of all Americans are made without reference to the desires or concerns of those people. These decisions are, in fact, often made without any reference to the needs of the nation or any community within the nation.

If competitiveness is not to be based on low-wage, corner-cutting strategies that undermine wages, working conditions, consumer safety, and the environment, then there will have to be a coordinated, considered attempt to devise other ways to develop the economy. Mechanisms that encourage the traditional components of competitiveness—savings, capital investment, industrial innovation, infrastructure development, work-force skills, and work effort—are not enough.[31] A national development plan must also be dedicated to creating new jobs and to upgrading the jobs that are already available. Moreover, an industrial or development plan should not be limited to business stimulation per se. Productivity growth also requires public investment in social infrastructure, such as health care and education.[32] Furthermore, it should have as a goal "sus-

TOOLBOX 4.6

PROGRAM FOR A DEMOCRATIC ECONOMY

PROGRAM THEMES	PROGRAM PROPOSALS
■ Right to economic security and equity	Public jobs programs Significantly higher minimum wage Reduced workweek and work sharing Pay equity and renewed affirmative action Expanded child care, family-leave programs Lower real interest rates
■ Right to a democratic workplace	A worker's bill of rights Labor law reform to promote democratically controlled unions Plant-closing legislation Public support for profit-sharing and workers' cooperatives Workers' right to know
■ Right to chart our economic futures	Democratize Federal Reserve Board Investment bank for democratic allocation of capital Managed trade for balanced growth Expanded infrastructural investment Local communities' environmental bill of rights Local right-to-know legislation
■ Right to a better way of life	Dramatically reduced military spending National health insurance program Closing of nuclear power plants; expansion of public support for renewable energy Expanded public support for decent, low-cost housing Expanded public support for education Increased tax rates on upper-income people

SOURCE: Samuel Bowles, David M. Gordon, and Thomas E. Weisskopf, *After the Waste Land: A Democratic Economics for the Year 2000* (Armonk, NY: M.E. Sharpe Inc., 1990).

tainable productivity growth" so that the effects on the natural environment are controlled and resources are conserved.[33]

Most important, however, an industrial policy that truly advances the cause of equity will have democratic roots and be implemented through democratic practice.[34] If it is not so structured, there is a danger that an industrial policy would skew the balance of economic and political power even further toward the corporate elite and away from workers, small businesses, and grassroots activists. But an industrial policy that is informed by the desires, needs, and decisions of the grassroots can help to guarantee the rights of all citizens to a decent living under dignified conditions, while ending their dependency on the caprice of profit-driven employers.

What are the goals that might shape such a plan? What goals might unite the various groups—unionists, nonunion workers, women's and ethnic organizations, environmentalists, community groups, and progressive religious organizations—involved in struggles for equitable economic development? To make this country a decent place to live for both current and future generations, the following objectives seem essential:

- secure, safe, and meaningful jobs at fair and livable wages;
- adequate, reliable, and accessible health care and education;
- governments and corporations that act responsibly toward us and our communities and that are accountable to us;
- sustainable, equitable, and democratic development; and
- international trade and investment policies that protect and advance labor rights, environmental standards, and community health and safety.

Playing Hard Ball in the Global Arena

Transnational corporations (TNCs) seek profits and freedom. As the case studies in Chapter 2 suggested, TNCs often have little commitment to the health of local (or state or national) economies or to the livelihoods of the people who live within them. Moreover, the pressures of poverty, underdevelopment, and economic decline mean there are always other communities and other countries offering attractive packages of wage, tax, and regulatory concessions. As a result, TNCs are able to play workers and communities in all countries against one another. The only way to even the score—to make TNCs more socially accountable, both at home and abroad—is to include the global playing field in strategies for change. The rules that govern corporate behavior in one country must be as strict as those in the next, and they must be intended to protect and enhance the standing of workers, communities, and the planet, not just profits.

To achieve these goals, international mechanisms are needed that enable workers to resist government and corporate competitive strategies based on low wages, benefits, and standards. Multilateral controls on capital to require social accountability are necessary. These mechanisms and objectives should be built into trade agreements and into other institutions and accords that govern the international political economy.

In addition, the intention to upgrade both the status of workers and their living conditions should be reflected in the commitments that nation-states make on the international scene. Ratifying the labor rights conventions of the International Labor Organization and the international human rights conventions of the United Nations are important steps to be taken in order to begin the long process of harmonizing international labor standards and working conditions in an upward direction. The United States must also improve its enforcement of laws requiring trading partners to uphold international labor standards if they receive trade concessions or other assistance from this country.

These lofty objectives are the components of an international political economy based on equity, security, development, and democracy. To achieve them, the United States will need an energetic and principled international strategy headed by visionary national leaders who aim to serve the interests of the poor, the working class (broadly defined), and future generations both in this country and abroad. But government officials and corporate leaders cannot be the only players in the game. International grassroots and worker organization is a necessity if popular interests are to be served and if economic democracy is to be enhanced.

Organize and Mobilize

Transnational citizen networks are needed in order to put the brakes on the unregulated movement of capital and to force companies to be responsible to their workers and communities.[35] International consumer boycotts, transboundary union campaigns and solidarity efforts, and issue-focused movements (such as the U.S.-

Mexico coalitions mobilized against NAFTA) help both to inform international partners about the conditions faced by counterparts abroad and to mobilize united fronts against irresponsible corporate behavior. Even if adequate laws were on the books and pro-people and pro-environment trade and investment policies were in place, networks like these would be important to prod corporations and governments to comply with their commitments. The transnational consumer boycott against Nestlé products, for example, forced the corporation to revise the way it marketed its infant formula and led the United Nations to attempt to develop a code of conduct for TNCs. Organized pressure from below, from locations around the world that are the production sites and markets for TNCs and the source of votes for government leaders, is a prerequisite for the substantive economic and political changes needed to resolve problems like runaways.

As long as companies can cross borders looking for cheaper labor costs and lax regulations, workers and communities everywhere will be disadvantaged—unless workers and communities everywhere find ways to join together in common efforts to bring wages and working conditions up to levels that provide for a dignified and secure life. In the past few years, progressive unionists in the United States and abroad have begun working toward this goal. The strategies, tactics, and linkages they are creating may be laying the foundation for global economic democracy.

At a 1990 conference of unionists in Miami, activists articulated a "one-world strategy" that parallels the global strategies of transnational corporations.[36] Treating the world as an interconnected and interdependent whole, the one-world strategy calls for transboundary organizing of workers and other popular forces in a coalition aimed at upgrading the world's living and working conditions. "We recognize that international economic integration will continue, and that wages and working conditions will equalize," said Ron Blackwell, an economist with the Amalgamated Clothing and Textile Workers Union. "The task is to build international worker solidarity to assure that wages and working conditions tend to equalize at a higher rather than lower level."[37]

Connected by fax machines, electronic mail, and satellite links, workers around the world who work for the same corporations are able to share information about their employers and even to mount international direct actions like strikes and community efforts like boycotts. In some cases, they can work through the international trade secretariat to which their union is affiliated, thus gaining the

TOOLBOX 4.7

HANDS ACROSS THE BORDER

Mexico has been one of the most important battlegrounds in U.S. labor's struggle to keep jobs from moving abroad. Low wages, minimal regulations, a largely unorganized work force, and geographic proximity have made Mexican maquiladoras irresistibly attractive to many U.S.-based manufacturers. But these same characteristics have also made Mexico an excellent place for U.S. unions to begin to develop a more effective international strategy.

Until the early 1990s, however, the AFL-CIO neglected organizing south of the border, often supporting conservative unions linked to the Mexican government. The proposed North American Free Trade Agreement (NAFTA) ended labor's inaction. A number of union officials recognized that political activity within the United States was only half of the response that NAFTA required. The anti-NAFTA coalitions of labor, environmental, consumer, and other groups represented exciting new possibilities in the United States, but, as the political director of the United Electrical Workers (UE) told *Dollars and Sense*, "Much of the work in those coalitions is ultimately legislative. We don't think that's enough. . . In the last ten years, [the UE] has lost 10,000 jobs to Mexico alone. The answer that too often gets ignored by the labor movement is solidarity across borders."

To begin moving toward transboundary labor solidarity, unionists in each country need to get to know their counterparts and the circumstances they face. A few unionists gained a head start by participating in a series of bi- and trinational exchanges launched in 1988. Sponsored by a small, New York-based group called Mexico-U.S. Diálogos, the exchanges brought together North American counterparts from different social sectors to share perspectives, problems, and ideas for the future.

Other U.S. unions have made contacts through efforts to link NAFTA opponents across North America. At an October 1991 trinational anti-NAFTA meeting in Zacatecas, Mexico, for example, UE representatives met officials of the Authentic Labor Front (FAT). The two groups have since embarked on the most concrete example of U.S.-Mexican labor solidarity to date, agreeing to cooperate in organizing maquiladora workers. The effort is focusing on runaway plants that started up in Mexico after shutting down UE-represented shops in the United States. Other unions, including the Communications Workers of America and the Service Employees International Union, have also set up contacts with Mexican unionists.

Another joint effort sprang from labor violations—a practice all too common in Mexico. After the murder of a Mexican Ford worker in January 1990, several of his co-workers traveled to the United States and Canada seeking support from the United Auto Workers (UAW) and the Canadian Auto Workers. The Canadians and a couple of UAW locals—in St. Paul, Minnesota, and Kansas City, Missouri—launched publicity campaigns and encouraged their members to write both Ford's corporate headquarters and the Mexican government. Delegations of U.S. and Canadian auto workers traveled to Cuautitlán—just north of Mexico City—to meet with the dissidents and to leaflet at the plant's gates. Officials of the St. Paul local publicly challenged Ford executives to explain the company's apparent violation of basic labor rights in Mexico. The activists caused enough trouble for Ford in the United States that the company demanded that Mexican unionists—who had been fired as part of Ford's strike-breaking effort—cut their ties to U.S. groups before they could receive their severance pay.

In addition to building direct contacts and forging joint strategies with cross-border counterparts, a second international labor strategy involves the establishment of enforceable minimum labor standards. Enforcing existing laws is a first step in this process. In the United States, this means using the provisions of the 1984 Trade and Tariff Act that require countries to meet internationally recognized minimum labor standards in order to gain duty-free access to the U.S. market for their goods.

In 1991 a group of U.S. activists filed a petition with the U.S. Trade Representative (USTR) requesting that Mexican exports be denied eligibility for duty-free treatment, based on the violation of workers' rights at the Ford plant in Cuautitlán, among other cases. The USTR rejected the petition out of hand, illegally failing to detail reasons. "How do you overlook the fact that Mexican workers are routinely fired, beaten, disappeared, shot, and even killed for exercising their right to democratic trade unionism?" asked petitioner and Ford worker Tom Laney in a letter to then-USTR Carla Hills.

The trade office's rejection of the petition highlighted the difficulty of relying on individual nations to enforce international labor rights. The process as it is now structured is hostage to the political priorities of the U.S. executive branch. But labor-rights activists argue that only by bringing cases, filing suits, and demonstrating the system's ineffectiveness will they be able to push the issue onto the national agenda. And only by working closely with labor organizations around the globe will activists be able to build trust, incorporate concerns, and create an international movement to include labor rights in international trade and investment agreements.

advantage of a global network of unionists that can be mobilized behind common actions.

Unionists are not the only ones involved in efforts like these. Transnational worker-community coalitions are focusing on a variety of problems related to globalization, most aiming to achieve some measure of control over corporate behavior. The Coalition for Justice in the Maquiladoras, for instance, is a binational association of religious, environmental, labor, Latino, and women's organizations that concentrates its efforts on maquiladoras along the U.S.-Mexico border. The coalition has formulated a code of conduct to promote corporate social responsibility in the maquiladora industry. Asserting that "moral behavior knows no borders," the coalition proposes that U.S. companies operating maquiladoras observe U.S. and Mexican environmental regulations, observe basic worker rights, and support community infrastructure needs.[38]

But the coalition goes beyond just proposing that corporations help to alleviate the critical problems that their activities create. It also mounts corporate campaigns against notorious violators. By generating publicity about inadequate environmental or health and safety practices, by calling for shareholder resolutions requiring companies to adhere to the coalition's standards of conduct, and by conducting visitor exchanges so that U.S. citizens can see the conditions under which Mexicans on the border live and work, the coalition continually prods maquila owners to adopt socially responsible business practices.

Such international efforts will need to be the wave of the future as the fight continues against runaways, deindustrialization, and the lack of corporate accountability. If not, transnational corporations will simply continue to skip country to country, placing workers and communities around the world in competition for investment.

Socially Responsible Trade Policies

In an era of globalization, devising an appropriate trade policy is a fundamental requirement of any successful program to save and create good jobs. Over the long term at least, decentralized local initiatives and inward-looking national strategies cannot win against runaways if one's national economy is integrated into an unregulated global market. When unfettered trade and investment relations link partners with great disparities in the conditions under which goods and services are produced, free trade puts extreme pressure on the country with higher labor, environmental, and consumer-safety standards to lower those standards. If the borders remain open, if corporate decisions to relocate are left unregulated, and if the country with higher standards insists on keeping standards high, a dual process is unleashed that wipes out jobs. On the one hand, cheap imports produced by low-wage workers in a lax regulatory environment sweep across the border, eroding the market share of domestically produced goods. On the other hand, corporations seeking to survive or to pump up their profits close up shop and move abroad to take advantage of lower costs. Rather than face the loss of jobs to such processes, governments and workers alike will often agree to slash regulations, wages, and benefits in order to attract investment. Neither jobs nor accountability are preserved in the long run, and TNCs get more powerful while the public right to chart the country's economic future is gradually transferred into the hands of corporate leaders.

Instead of capitulating to such pressures, trade policies should be designed to force wages, working conditions, and environmental standards up, not down. Failing that, trade policies should at least be designed to protect the rights of workers and communities to decent working and living conditions and to set standards regulating the operations of corporations in their localities. As Thea Lee, an analyst at the Washington-based Economic Policy Institute, explained, "We need to be able to regulate the goods that come across our border if we want to continue to regulate our domestic environment and workplace. To that end, we should restrict the import of goods produced in a way that is morally or legally reprehensible."[39] In other words, if goods are produced with child labor, poverty wages, or by polluting the environment, they should not be allowed to cross the border without penalty.

There are already precedents for such restrictions. Over the decade of the 1980s, various U.S. trade laws were written to include requirements that trading partners must observe fundamental labor rights.[40] Some of this legislation applies to countries that receive preferential trade benefits under special U.S. trade promotion programs. Participation in programs like the Generalized System of Preferences and the Caribbean Basin Initiative, for example, are conditioned on the recipient government's protection of five internationally recognized worker rights.[41] Likewise, the Omnibus Trade and Competitiveness Act of 1988 allows the U.S. president to impose retaliatory duties upon or deny U.S.

market access to products from countries that deny worker rights. Similar obligations apply to countries that participate in the export-promotion programs of the Overseas Private Investment Corporation. Unfortunately, these provisions are not well-enforced, but they are certainly potentially useful and they indicate some acceptance of the need to use trade policy as a tool to further the advancement of international worker rights.

One enforcement provision that has been suggested is the "social tariff."[42] Such a tariff would be levied against goods from countries that gained a competitive advantage either by holding wages and working conditions below a certain standard or from low environmental protection standards or lax enforcement of environmental laws. A social tariff would tax away the cost advantages of producers who benefited from such lax enforcement of labor rights and environmental protections. In principle, the tariff would be equal to that portion of the difference in final cost between producers of equivalent products that could be attributed to differences in policies regarding such matters as the rights of labor to work under reasonably acceptable conditions and the right of communities to quality environments.[43]

Obviously, restrictions like these could have sharply negative repercussions on trading partners that depend on trade with the United States but that do not observe minimum worker rights. Economic downturns in those countries certainly hurt workers and their communities. How can such policies be made to advance the objective of mutual, equitable development? They must be packaged with appropriate development strategies and efforts to reform the development policies of institutions like the World Bank and the International Monetary Fund. These bodies promote the same free-market, export-oriented development strategy that now holds favor in many governments and corporations. But export-driven development policies encourage wage and benefit slashing, regulation bashing, and worker repression in order to keep the cost of exports low enough to compete effectively on the world market. Another problem is that the international lending institutions emphasize debt repayment and austerity measures, which siphon economic resources out of third world countries and into the coffers of international financial institutions, reducing demand and slowing growth. By deemphasizing exports as an engine of growth, by revitalizing efforts to build domestic industries and domestic markets, and by providing substantive debt relief, development policies can be made to serve the world's majorities while trade policies encourage improvements in international worker rights.

People-Friendly Trade Agreements

International trade and investment agreements could be used to boost the position of labor and protect the environment if they were designed to do so. Mostly, however, they are set up to make it easier for capital, ideas, technology, products, and services to cross national boundaries, allowing the market to distribute the costs and benefits of the transactions.

But trade and investment agreements that rely on market forces to pay for social costs like job loss, persistent unemployment, and pollution are not likely to lead to equitable, democratic, and sustainable development. The market just does not handle social costs very well. After a decade of economic liberalization and deregulation in the United States and Mexico, for instance, falling real incomes, sharply increased poverty rates, rising long-term unemployment, widening gaps between rich and poor, infrastructure decay, and environmental deterioration raise serious questions about approaches to development based solely on the market. Competitive strategies based on low wages and feeble protections for workers have eroded living standards, undermined unions, and increased desperation, thus fueling the processes that support the runaway phenomenon. Even more of a concern, the potential for other nations to sign on to NAFTA and the existence of global agreements like GATT help to spread these economic strategies and their deficiencies throughout the hemisphere and around the world.

Rather than relying on the market to distribute costs and benefits, trade and investment agreements can be designed to make economic integration and expanding trade serve broader social values. Constructing agreements that explicitly aim to defend labor rights and working conditions, build (or rebuild) livable communities, safeguard the environment, and protect the public health requires mechanisms that guide market forces to compensate for problems generated by unrestricted development.[44]

First of all, the formulation of trade agreements must be forced out of the back rooms. Transparency, accountability, and public participation are prerequisites for a fully functioning economic and political system based on equity and sustainability. Because of the weighty decisions being made and their wide-ranging impacts, the formulation of agreements like NAFTA make it crucial that those who have traditionally been left out of the decisionmaking process advance their own agendas, projects, and alternatives in policy forums.

Getting into those policymaking arenas is the hard part. International agreements like GATT and NAFTA actually undermine democ-

TOOLBOX 4.8 **NORTH AMERICAN HEALTH, LABOR, AND ENVIRONMENTAL COMMISSION**

Achieving equitable and sustainable development in the global arena requires representative and accountable institutions that oversee international relationships. During the debates over NAFTA, activist organizations concerned with shaping a pro-people and pro-environment trade agreement suggested establishing a trinational commission (with fundraising and enforcement authority) that could monitor and find solutions to health, environmental, and labor issues.

If such a commission were to be established, it would need to be structured carefully. Otherwise, it could easily be dominated by individuals and organizations with vested interests in imposing the lowest possible restrictions on business and minimizing the power of affected communities. In addition—and this is probably the toughest problem—affected workers, their communities, and other activists would have to be organized well enough to articulate a coherent vision for the commission and be able to mobilize voters and supporters around candidates and issues.

To meet the tests of accountability, representativeness, and effectiveness, the following minimum requirements are crucial:

■ Representatives to the commission should be elected, not appointed, and participants should represent a range of important sectors such as labor, environmentalists, community activists, health-care providers, business associations, and consumer-protection groups. To ensure this range of participants, there might be a certain number of seats reserved for each sector.

■ A recall provision must be included so that participants on the commission can be removed if constituents do not feel that their interests are being served.

racy by taking important decisionmaking powers out of the hands of local, state, and national elected leaders and vesting them in unelected, unrepresentative, and unaccountable institutions.[45] As structured by the Bush and Salinas governments, for example, the Free Trade Commission mandated by NAFTA would include only government officials, although the panels set up to arbitrate disputes may include "experts" in international law and trade. Excluded, however,

■ To achieve transparency, the proceedings of the commission should be public, and documents, decisions, hearing dates, and the like must be readily available to all interested parties.

■ Governments should not be the only agents permitted to bring complaints before the commission. Workers, communities, environmentalists, and other affected parties must be able to raise complaints, present evidence, and seek resolution of grievances.

■ To assure independence, the commission must have fundraising mechanisms built into its structure. To minimize dependence on any one source of financing, commission funds should be derived from a combination of user fees, fines, taxes, and earmarked funding from government and community funds.

■ To enhance effectiveness, the commission must have enforcement powers, and NAFTA itself must include provisions specifically aimed at safeguarding and boosting the position of workers, communities, and the environment. NAFTA must also link violations of these provisions to sanctions that could be applied by the commission.

SOURCES: Interview with Karen Hansen-Kuhn, Development GAP, March 12, 1993; interview with Jim Benn, Federation for Industrial Retention and Renewal, March 4, 1993; Michael Gregory, "Environment, Sustainable Development, Public Participation and the NAFTA: A Retrospective," *Journal of Environmental Law and Litigation* (Aug. 1992); Proyecto Fronterizo de Educación Ambiental and Border Ecology Project, "The North American Free Trade Agreement: Environmental and Health Issues in the Interior of Mexico and Options for Environmental Safeguards" (Tijuana and Naco, AZ, Oct. 1992); and U.S. Congress, Office of Technology Assessment, *U.S.-Mexico Trade: Pulling Together or Pulling Apart?* (Washington, DC: Government Printing Office, Oct. 1992).

would be independent representatives from sectors like labor, consumers, and community groups who would often be better able to evaluate the effects of policy on their constituents. Negotiations held in secret and disputes settled behind closed doors do little to ensure that the needs and concerns of affected communities and interest groups are taken into account, much less protected.

In addition to ensuring democratic accountability, trade agreements must provide compensatory financing to sectors that are disadvantaged by the accords as well as to countries like Mexico that need extra resources in order to improve labor and environmental standards and enforcement. Without some sort of compensatory mechanism, these governments will be encouraged to continue competing for capital by keeping wages low and regulations lax, while workers and communities who lose their livelihoods as trade shifts jobs elsewhere may be unable to develop new employment options. A new regional institution might be established to provide such financing not only to Mexico, but to workers and communities in the United States (and Canada) as well, if they have been disadvantaged by the globalizing economy.[46] Under the terms of trade agreements, funding could be provided for worker training, retooling and other conversion investments, job creation in rural areas, health and safety programs, and the development and upward harmonization of norms, standards, and regulations.

Such funding must be accompanied by adequate controls, lest it be used to grease the rails for runaways while failing to finance development projects that improve the lives and skills of ordinary people.[47] There are already examples of such ill-advised programs, even without NAFTA. In universities and training institutions along the U.S.-Mexico border, U.S. government-funded instruction and technical assistance are helping to provide new technologies and train employees for the maquiladoras. These programs subsidize profits and encourage runaways, but do not provide mechanisms for upgrading Mexican labor standards or wages.[48]

Making sure that trade agreements satisfy the needs of workers, their communities, and the environment also requires effective and accountable institutions. Commissions that oversee trade relations, for instance, need to have participants from a broad range of affected groups, ranging from business associations to environmental activists and unionists. Institutions that incorporate grassroots input in practice (not merely in rhetoric) are essential if the process of economic integration is to cease fueling runaways and deindustrialization at the expense of workers and communities.

An International Ideal of Social Accountability

Another way to help fight the negative effects of globalization is to ratify and enforce international legal codes that reflect a commitment to working people and the environment. These agreements, like the United Nations conventions on civil, political, economic, social, and cultural rights, indicate priorities, aspirations, and commitments. Internationally recognized labor rights, such as those incorporated in conventions of the International Labor Organization, assert the rights of workers to organize, bargain collectively, and be protected against forced labor and unacceptable working conditions. There are many options for such agreements, ranging from those with rather specific objectives—like devising a "code of conduct" for transnational corporations—to those with very broad-ranging agendas like a North American social and environmental charter.[49]

International agreements bind the signatory governments to follow policies that are consistent with the goals outlined in the accords. If constructed with adequate enforcement mechanisms, such as an international court and trade sanctions, international frameworks could provide vehicles for nations, nongovernmental organizations, communities, and citizens to pursue legal judgments outside domestic court systems when provisions of the agreements are violated. Finally, when devised so that trade and investment policies are linked to social issues, international accords can help ensure that the effects of one upon the other are considered in tandem and not artificially separated.

Unfortunately, the United States has not ratified many of these conventions, preferring to set its own standards and to steer clear of international enforcement and regulation. But there are many pragmatic reasons for signing on to these international agreements. Fighting runaways and deindustrialization means fighting to keep good jobs. Because of globalization, that battle cannot be confined to just one country. More than ever, being able to retain family-wage jobs in the United States requires raising living standards abroad. Failure to enforce international worker rights can reduce the competitiveness of countries that already have high standards or that are contemplating stricter standards. The downward pressure on wages and working conditions that results from unenforced rights could decrease global aggregate demand, leading to increased unemployment and excess capacity worldwide. These symptoms threaten the health of the global economy as a whole, and because national economies are so intermeshed with the international one, the negative repercussions would ripple throughout the world.[50]

TOOLBOX 4.9

OF TRADE AGREEMENTS AND SOCIAL CHARTERS

During the negotiation of the North American Free Trade Agreement (NAFTA), many critics of the pact raised concerns that the dropping of trade barriers would lead to a decline in labor and environmental standards in all three countries. They urged the governments of the United States, Canada, and Mexico to consider implementing a "social and environmental charter" patterned on a similar document created by the members of the European Community.

Such a charter would include a set of enforceable threshold protections for labor and the environment that would be binding on all parties to NAFTA. This would help reduce variations in regulations and enforcement so that parties with weaker standards would not gain a competitive edge in the bidding war for foreign investment. Better still, a more ambitious charter could help to institute vehicles for worker and community participation in economic decisionmaking—through international work councils, for example—and could move to harmonize standards in an upward direction over the course of a given phase-in period.

Some components of a charter for North America might include:

■ support for internationally recognized worker rights, such as the right to freedom of association; the right to bargain collectively; prohibitions against the use of forced labor; guidelines on the use of child labor; and equal protection for all workers regardless of nationality, race, age, gender, or religion;

■ minimum continental labor standards, such as occupational health and safety regulations, and a commitment to raising continental wage levels within a specified time period;

■ recognition of new labor rights, such as the right to move freely throughout the region in search of employment as well as equal protection for workers regardless of sexual preference;

■ minimum continental environmental standards, including protection of biospheres and natural resources; requirements for community and

International labor standards can help prevent international competition from undermining national labor legislation. In addition, international worker rights can help set limits on the strategies firms and governments can use to cut wages and stimulate exports. Global standards can also help to foster increases in the wages of workers in other countries, thus boosting consumption and global economic

workplace right-to-know provisions; prohibitions on the export of toxic and hazardous substances banned in the country of origin; requirements that industries reduce and minimize the amount and toxicity of hazardous substances that they use; and requirements that businesses demonstrate compliance with pollution-control and pollution-abatement standards;

■ provisions to enhance worker and community involvement in economic decisionmaking, including requirements that businesses consult in advance with workers and communities about plans to restructure or relocate operations; the creation of institutions to guide and oversee trade that include representatives of labor, environmental organizations, and community groups as voting members; and requirements that workers be allowed to organize and bargain collectively across national boundaries;

■ a strengthened social safety net, including adequate levels of social security benefits; fair and adequate unemployment compensation; access to adequate and reliable health care; access to a decent education; and adequate training for displaced workers to prepare them for family-wage jobs;

■ provisions that guarantee the rights of national, state, and local governments to legislate protections that are higher than the negotiated minimum standards agreed upon by signatory countries; and

■ a commitment to exploring supranational possibilities for overseeing and enforcing the charter's provisions.

SOURCES: George E. Brown Jr., J. William Goold, and John Cavanagh, "Making Trade Fair," *World Policy Journal* (Spring 1992); Cuauhtémoc Cárdenas, "The Continental Development and Trade Initiative" (Speech given before the Americas Society, New York, Feb. 8, 1991); U.S. Congress, Office of Technology Assessment, *U.S.-Mexico Trade: Pulling Together or Pulling Apart* (Washington, DC: Government Printing Office, Oct. 1992); and "The Social Charter Implications of the NAFTA," *Canada-U.S. Outlook* 3, no. 3 (Aug. 1992).

growth. Given the integration of the global economy, individual nations cannot go it alone in terms of enforcement or regulation. Rather, a commitment on the international level is necessary, accompanied by protections in national trade and investment policies. International commitment puts each country that ratifies the agreement on the same footing as other signers, at least as far as recognized obligations to improving global living and working conditions are concerned. Such a commitment makes it harder for corporations to play one country against another, and it provides an opportunity for countries that have ratified the agreements to bring a case against others that have also committed to the conventions but are not fulfilling their obligations.

Not all such agreements need to be global in scope. On the contrary, binational or multilateral accords are essential to improving conditions for workers and communities, especially among close trading partners like the United States and Mexico. Both Mexican labor activists and immigrant rights advocates in both countries have been pushing for the U.S. and Mexican governments to negotiate agreements on labor mobility, for instance, that would include the right of workers to move freely across the border in search of employment. Likewise, organizations like the American Friends Service Committee and the Centro de Estudios Fronterizos y de Promoción de los Derechos Humanos (Center for Border Studies and Human Rights) are seeking adequate human rights protections for Mexican workers residing legally or illegally in the United States.

With respect to the United States and Mexico, the most extensive proposal to emerge from considerations of corporate accountability and stronger standards has been for a social charter modeled on the one passed by the European Community as part of its own integration process.[51] A North American social and environmental charter would commit the signatory governments gradually to standardize norms relating to issues like labor rights, migration, and the environment. Linked to NAFTA or some similar trade agreement, the charter would be designed to ensure that the conditions under which people live and work in the North American countries would be harmonized in an upward direction and not allowed to deteriorate as part of the bidding war for capital.

Competition, Solidarity, and the Stakes of the Game

RUNAWAY AMERICA IS NOT JUST THE story of one country, nor even that of one continent. The trends and pressures described in this book affect communities and people all over the world. *Runaway America* describes a syndrome of deindustrialization, deregulation, plant closures, job loss, and wage cutbacks that hurt working people and the communities in which they live, while loosening controls over capital. No country is immune to these pressures, even if, at any given moment, that country is the destination, and not the source, of runaway investment. Just as Mexico has already lost jobs and investment to lower-wage sites in Asia, Central America, and the Caribbean, so are other countries and communities subject to the ebb and flow of foreign investment. As long as these communities are tied into the global economy, as long as the rules of that economy favor capital mobility over corporate accountability, and as long as investment decisions are made with the single purpose of raising profits, grassroots gains from globalization cannot be permanent.

The current rules of the international economy make winners out of a few big corporations and losers out of the majority of the world's workers and communities. But the process of global economic integration need not hold only peril for the world's communities. On the contrary, globalization could promise many benefits. Globalization links suppliers, producers, workers, and consumers in far-flung locations. Properly structured, economic integration could make it possible to have economic security through trade and foreign investment even when complete self-sufficiency is impossible due to a lack of resources or to a desire for goods and information produced elsewhere. Economic integration also spurs political integration because it creates a need for overarching rules to govern the system. In addition, it facilitates communication among people in different places, especially if they work for or buy from the same companies. As a consequence, globalization offers both a reason for and a means to develop a common political agenda for working people and communities who wish to change the rules guiding national and international economies.

Debate over NAFTA has offered a critical opening for progressive labor-community coalitions that wish to shape economic integration and find the terms of a common political agenda. Because the trade accord threatens to increase runaways but fails to incorporate mechanisms to protect labor rights, wages, working conditions, the environment, or community health and safety, it has stimulated both concern and activism throughout North America. Its anticipated wide-reaching effects in all three countries have sparked the formation of several broad-based, transboundary coalitions. Among these are the North American Worker-to-Worker Network, and the trilateral meetings held by the Action Canada Network, Mexican Free Trade Network, and the U.S. Alliance for Responsible Trade. These organizations are working to incorporate within the text of the accord enforceable, minimum standards for protecting workers, communities, and the environment. As a vehicle for exploring, explaining, and mobilizing around globalization and its effects, NAFTA provides one of the best opportunities in history to press for changes to international trade and investment policies that will serve workers and communities and move the continent toward economic democracy.

But just working on NAFTA or on other international trade issues is not enough. It is unlikely that trade negotiators will adopt policies that are more progressive than the national political climate. Without strong national policies and public consensus about the direction of the economy, effective international trade policies will likely not get written, much less enforced. Labor and community activists who are concerned about these issues will have to educate and organize the larger population, as well as policymakers. Initiatives like NAFTA may be the opening wedge for such discussions, but processes like runaways and deindustrialization occur—and will continue to occur—with or without a free trade agreement. Making it clear that these problems are generated largely by rules favoring corporate freedom over the needs of workers and communities is the more important—and more difficult—part of the organizing effort.

As part of the task ahead, simplistic solutions like protectionism and "Buy American" strategies will have to be reconsidered and revamped, or jettisoned altogether. Protectionist policies in the form of a social tariff to enforce principles like internationally recognized labor rights may, if carefully constructed, serve to nudge global standards regarding labor and the environment in an upward direction. But all too often, protectionism does nothing to advance worker or community rights. Rather, protectionist policies often shelter corporations that guard their own freedom with a vengeance while squeezing concessions and incentives out of their workers and local governments in the name of enhancing "competitiveness."

On an international level, protectionism erects barriers of ill will between workers in each country who are forced by global processes and corporate strategies to compete with each other for investment and jobs. The result is isolation from counterparts abroad who are passengers in the same global economic boat and should be natural allies. Competition among the world's communities and their workers is not the answer to runaways. On the contrary, such competition helps to keep capital footloose and governments nonresponsive to the needs of labor. Equitable, sustainable, and democratic development cannot result under these conditions.

The history of the past three decades of runaways and deindustrialization shows that the process of globalization must be shaped in order to distribute its costs and benefits broadly and equitably. This is necessary not only to defend the living standards of working people in the industrialized countries, but to raise the wages and living conditions of people in the developing world. Public policies and institutions that regulate globalization in the interests of people and the environment are needed, whether instituted at the local level or globally.

Unfortunately, there are no blueprints to guide activists toward solutions to these problems. But what seems clear is that democratic controls on capital mobility are required so that corporations will not be able to play workers and communities against one another in search of the most concessionary business climate. Workers and communities should aim to get "not just a bigger piece of the pie, but a piece of the kitchen," insists Jim Benn of the Federation for Industrial Retention and Renewal.

Getting a piece of the kitchen means shifting the center of power over economic decisions away from corporate elites and toward the grassroots. This is more than a prescription based on moral values; it has pragmatic roots. The labor, resources, ideas, and leadership of everyday people in everyday communities are needed to make and buy products and to provide and purchase services. If equitable, sustainable development is ever to be achieved, their participation in economic planning and decisionmaking is essential. That participation should be both one of the goals and one of the strategies of those working to confront the negative effects of globalization. Corporate accountability cannot be achieved without it.

References

Introduction

1. Runaways describe a particular type of plant movement. It is not an expansion of operations abroad to penetrate new markets or to make use of natural resources, transportation links, or the other possible advantages of the new site. Instead, runaway plants are those that curtail or close down production in one location in order to move to a more advantageous site, usually in search of lower costs of production. In the United States, a very wide range of businesses are closing down to relocate abroad, including factories, offices, shops, stores, and warehouses. For the sake of convenience, we refer to all such establishments as "plants."
2. The Enterprise for the Americas Initiative, proposed by President George Bush in 1990, envisions a free trade zone based on free-market principles that would include the entire Western Hemisphere.

Chapter 1

1. For a critical overview of the Bretton Woods system, described by the authors as "Wall Street Internationalism," see Daniel Cantor and Juliet Schor, *Tunnel Vision: Labor, the World Economy, and Central America* (Boston: South End Press, 1987). For a wider-ranging study of the institutions that served to structure capitalist relations in the United States after World War II, see the provocative and well-argued analysis of Samuel Bowles, David M. Gordon, and Thomas E. Weisskopf, *After the Waste Land: A Democratic Economics for the Year 2000* (Armonk, NY: M.E. Sharpe Inc., 1990), pp. 47-79. Also see John Gerard Ruggie, "International Regimes, Transactions, and Change: Embedded Liberalism in the Postwar Economic Order," *International Organization* 36 (1982), and Robert Gilpin, *The Political Economy of International Relations* (Princeton, NJ: Princeton University Press, 1987), pp. 131-42.
2. For discussions of GATT and NAFTA and the potential ways in which they could be used to preempt strict national standards on environmental protection, see: Walter Russell Mead, "Bushism, Found: A Second-Term Agenda Hidden in Trade Agreements," *Harper's*, Sept. 1992; Robert Schaeffer, "Trading Away the Planet," in John Cavanagh et al., eds., *Trading Freedom: How Free Trade Affects Our Lives, Work and Environment* (San Francisco: The Institute for Food and Development Policy, 1992), pp. 27-31; "Coming to Terms with Trade," *Environmental Action* 24, no. 2 (Summer 1992), pp. 31-36; and Michael Gregory, "Environment, Sustainable Development, Public Participation and the NAFTA: A Retrospective," *Journal of Environmental Law and Litigation* (Aug. 1992).
3. This tendency to move abroad in pursuit of higher profit rates is reinforced by probusiness economic philosophies that hold corporate health to be the key to national prosperity. Roughly translated in the common vernacular as, "What's good for General Motors is good for the country," these philosophies underlie policies that protect high profit rates and corporate freedom, even when those benefits to business are not productively reinvested in

local communities. Answers to problems like runaways therefore lie in changing the faulty economic ideology that dominates policymaking and the rules of the international economy, not in expecting corporations to behave differently under the current rules. Even under the current rules, however, long-term corporate health cannot be guaranteed through globalization processes that are dependent on low-wage labor because excess capacity and sluggish demand will threaten corporate viability in the long run.

4. Comprehensive descriptions of the changing U.S. economy can be found in Donald Barlett and James Steele, *America: What Went Wrong?* (Kansas City: Andrews and McMeel, 1992); Bennett Harrison and Barry Bluestone, *The Great U-Turn: Corporate Restructuring and the Polarizing of America* (New York: Basic Books, 1988); and Juliet Schor, *The Overworked American: The Unexpected Decline of Leisure* (New York: Basic Books, 1991). See also the Economic Policy Institute's voluminous collection of employment and wage data for the decade: Lawrence Mishel and Jared Bernstein, *Declining Wages for High School and College Graduates: Pay and Benefits Trends by Education, Gender, Occupation, and State, 1979-1991* (Washington, DC: Economic Policy Institute, 1992), and Lawrence Mishel and David M. Frankel, *The State of Working America 1990-91* (Armonk, NY: M.E. Sharpe Inc., 1991).

5. With after-tax profits falling fairly steadily since the mid-1960s, slashing labor costs has proven to be the quickest way to hike profits. For information on the decline of the after-tax profit rate of U.S. corporations since the 1960s, see: Bowles et al., *After the Waste Land* (see chap. 1, n. 1), pp. 43-45, 77-79, 157-61; Barry Bluestone and Bennett Harrison, *The Deindustrialization of America: Plant Closings, Community Abandonment, and the Dismantling of Basic Industry* (New York: Basic Books, 1982), pp. 147-49; and Robert B. Reich, *The Work of Nations: Preparing Ourselves for 21st-Century Capitalism* (New York: Alfred A. Knopf, 1991), p. 75-76.

6. Barlett and Steele, *America: What Went Wrong?* (see chap. 1, n. 4), p. 18.

7. Lawrence Mishel has determined that manufacturing's share of the gross domestic product declined sharply after 1973. According to Mishel's calculations, the share of GDP held by manufacturing fell from 24 percent in 1973 to 22.5 percent in 1979 and to 20.8 percent in 1985, where it held steady at least until the date of his study. Lawrence R. Mishel, "The Late Great Debate on Deindustrialization," *Challenge*, Jan.-Feb. 1989.

8. Ronald Kwan, "Footloose and Country Free: Mobility Key to Capitalists' Power," *Dollars & Sense*, March 1991, p. 7.

9. A. Sivanandan, "The Global Market Place," *International Labour Reports* 36, Nov.-Dec. 1989, p. 9.

10. See the case study of relocation and corporate "blackmail" of workers to obtain concessions in John Gaventa, "Capital Flight and Workers," in Cavanagh et al., *Trading Freedom* (see chap. 1, n. 2), pp. 19-23.

11. See Kim Moody, *An Injury to All: The Decline of American Unionism* (London: Verso, 1988); Harrison and Bluestone, *The Great U-Turn* (see chap. 1, n. 4), especially the chapter on "Zapping Labor," pp. 21-52; Bowles et al., *After the Waste Land* (see chap. 1, n. 1), pp. 85-88; and Bluestone and Harrison, *The Deindustrialization of America* (see chap. 1, n. 5), pp. 164-70, 178-80. Organized labor in the United States has suffered in part because of its own failures, including flawed organizing strategies, the leadership's disengagement from the rank and file, excessive bureaucratization, corruption, encrusted ideological stands, undemocratic decisionmaking processes, and lack of militancy. For a close look at U.S. labor's own political, strategic, and organizing failures, see Moody, *An Injury to All*; Staughton Lynd, *The Fight Against Shutdowns: Youngstown's Steel Mill Closings* (San Pedro, CA: Singlejack Books, 1982); and Beth Sims, *Workers of the World Undermined: American Labor's Role in U.S. Foreign Policy* (Boston: South End Press, 1992).

12. The term comes from Bowles et al., *After the Waste Land* (see chap. 1, n. 1), p. 133.

13. Focusing on the role that domestic politics plays in undermining U.S. living conditions is not meant to suggest that concerns about international competitiveness are irrelevant to union-busting efforts. Competitiveness issues—such as the increasing share of the U.S. market captured by imports—feed the attack against labor and are used to justify it. Domestic policy choices, however, are extremely important in their own right and have served

to undermine, rather than to shore up, the position of workers and their communities in the interests of bolstering the position of large corporations and the wealthy. For close examinations of this transfer of wealth and power over the decade of the 1980s and the domestic political motivations behind it, see Bowles et al., *After the Waste Land* (see chap. 1, n. 1); Barlett and Steele, *America: What Went Wrong?* (see chap. 1, n. 4); and Mishel and Frankel, *The State of Working America* (see chap. 1, n. 4).

14. Estimates of the total number of jobs lost in a community and in supplier industries as a result of cutbacks or a shutdown by a given employer vary depending on the industry in question and its linkages to other industries in the production chain. Looking at the auto industry, U.S. government studies in the early 1980s found that one to two jobs were lost in supplier industries (steel, rubber, glass, and textiles, for example) for every job lost in the motor vehicle industry itself. See summaries in Bluestone and Harrison, *The Deindustrialization of America* (see chap. 1, n. 5), pp. 71-72. Another factor that influences the size of the "ripple effect" following a shutdown is the size and diversity of the community's economic base and the level of its dependence on the plant in question. A study of the 1987 closing of the GM plants in Norwood and Fairfield, Ohio, for example, found that at least three jobs were lost throughout the region for every one job lost at the plants. At the time of the closing, the GM plant in Norwood accounted for more than 40 percent of the city's jobs, and the two plants bought services and materials from nearly 1,400 suppliers in the region. Cited in Michael Wallace and Joyce Rothschild, "Plant Closings, Capital Flight, and Worker Dislocation: The Long Shadow of Deindustrialization," in Michael Wallace and Joyce Rothschild, eds., *Deindustrialization and the Restructuring of American Industry*, vol. 3 of *Research in Politics and Society* (Greenwich, CT: JAI Press, 1988).

15. See, for example, Barlett and Steele, *America: What Went Wrong?* (see chap. 1, n. 4).

16. When all pretax incomes are ranked according to size, the median falls smack in the middle. That is, half the incomes are above and half below the median.

17. These figures are given in 1989 dollars and come from Mishel and Frankel, *The State of Working America* (see chap. 1, n. 4), pp. 12-15. Also see Philip Mattera, *Prosperity Lost* (Reading, MA: Addison-Wesley Publishing Company, Inc., 1990).

18. Mishel and Frankel, *The State of Working America* (ibid.), p. 15.

19. On the loss of leisure time and the rise in hours worked, see ibid. and Schor, *The Overworked American* (see chap. 1, n. 4).

20. Reich, *The Work of Nations* (see chap. 1, n. 5), p. 6.

21. U.S. Department of Labor, *Economic Adjustment and Worker Dislocation in a Competitive Society: Report of the Secretary of Labor's Task Force on Economic Adjustment and Worker Dislocation* (Washington, DC, Dec. 1986), and U.S. Congress, Office of Technology Assessment, *Technology and Structural Unemployment: Reemploying Displaced Adults*, OTA-ITE-250 (Washington, DC, Feb. 1986). The Bureau of Labor Statistics defines "displaced" workers as those who permanently lost their jobs after at least three years in the position. See also Michael Podgursky, *Estimated Losses Due to Job Displacement: Evidence from the Displaced Worker Surveys* (Washington, DC: Economic Policy Institute, April 1991).

22. Lisa Oppenheim, "Introduction," *Labor Research Review*, no. 19 (Fall 1992).

23. Edward E. Leamer, "Wage Effects of a U.S.-Mexican Free Trade Agreement" (Paper presented at the Mexico-U.S. FTA Conference, Brown University, Oct. 1991), Figure 4.

24. The only exception is in the textile industry, where maquiladoras are required to be 51-percent Mexican-owned. Assuming that the North American Free Trade Agreement is approved, this provision will be phased out.

25. To be labeled "Made in America," a product imported from the maquiladoras must receive "final processing" in the United States. The action of stamping the product "Made in America" is frequently the only "final processing" such goods receive in this country.

26. One of the first to move was Form-O-Uth, which manufactured brassieres for Sears in California and Texas. The company closed its California plant in 1969 when its maquiladora came on line in Reynosa, Tamaulipas. (The Texas plants were later closed when the company began operations in El Salvador.) In 1970 another Sears supplier, Warwick Electronics (owned by Whirlpool), opened a maquiladora in Tijuana. See Leslie Sklair, *The*

Maquiladoras: Present Status, Future Potential (Study submitted to the U.S. Office of Technology Assessment, Dec. 1991). Sklair describes Sears' campaign on pp. 50-52 and 131. Sklair cites James Worthy, *Shaping an American Institution: Robert E. Wood and Sears, Roebuck* (Urbana, IL: University of Illinois Press, 1984).

27. Customs officials record imports that qualify for duty-free status in two tariff lines now called HTS 9802.00.60 and 9802.00.80. These lines correspond to the pre-1990 tariff lines called TSUS 806.30 and 807.00. The total value of U.S. imports from Mexico under 806.30 and 807.00 in 1968 was $73 million. Since the proportion of nondutiable, U.S.-made components and materials in maquila exports to the United States has held fairly constant at just over 50 percent over the years, we have estimated roughly $40 million in duty-free exports in 1968. See Sklair, *The Maquiladoras: Present Status, Future Potential* (ibid.), p. 12.

28. The legislation governing these duty-free import policies is the Offshore Assembly Provision of U.S. tariff law. Existing in various forms since 1930, this provision allows firms to import goods without paying duties on any U.S.-made components or materials that were used to produce those goods. Note that Mexico's portion of the duty-free total of imports under TSUS 806.30 and 807.00 varies greatly from its portion of total imports under these codes. This is because Mexican maquiladoras use a much higher proportion of U.S.-made components in their assembly processes than do assemblers in developed countries such as Japan. As an illustration, in 1986 Mexico accounted for 18 percent of total imports under the Offshore Assembly Provision, but 54 percent of the duty-free portion of these imports.

29. Until Mexico adopted its General Law on Ecological Equilibrium and Environmental Protection in 1988, the country's environmental policies were inadequate to deal with the pressures of industrialization and were largely unenforced. See Stephen P. Mumme, C. Richard Bath, and Valerie J. Assetto, "Political Development and Environmental Policy in Mexico," *Latin American Research Review* 23, no. 1 (1988). Despite the improved legal framework resulting from the 1988 law, inadequate regulations and enforcement remain significant obstacles to environmental protection. Mexico has not consistently enforced its strong labor standards since 1940.

30. "History of Cost per Hour in Dollars," *Twin Plant News*, Aug. 1989, p. 56.

31. Business International Corp., *Succeeding in the New Mexico: Corporate Strategy, Globalization and the Free Trade Agreement* (New York, 1991), p. 187.

32. Data from Mexico's National Institute of Statistics, Geography, and Information (INEGI) and the Ministry of Programming and Budget (SPP), cited in ibid., p. 198. Making the increase in value added per employee even more impressive is the fact that real wages were lower in 1989 than in 1983. The wage rate is relevant because wages make up a large portion of value added in the maquiladoras.

Chapter 2

1. A plant-by-plant review of our list of runaways indicated that 167 work sites had lost over 73,000 jobs to Mexico in labor-intensive activities, while thirty-three sites had lost roughly 14,000 jobs in non-labor-intensive activities. For purposes of classification into one of these two groups we roughly estimated the contribution of direct labor to value added in the relevant portion of the production process. The figures vary slightly from those resulting from an industry-by-industry list such as Table 2.1 and should be considered more accurate.

2. By 1990 Foster Grant had reduced its turnover rate to an "acceptable" 100 percent. Sandy Tolan, "The Border Boom: Hope and Heartbreak," *New York Times Magazine*, July 1, 1990. It is possible, of course, that a more humanely organized work process would reduce overall training needs in the long term by reducing the turnover caused by the intense tedium of five-second cycle times.

3. The Volcker quote is from a hearing before the U.S. Senate Committee on Banking, Housing, and Urban Affairs, *Federal Reserve Policy Actions*, 96th Cong., Oct. 15, 1979. Galvin was

quoted in David Oliver Rolin, "Why Lost U.S. Jobs are Headed Abroad," *Scholastic Update*, Jan. 26, 1987. Walter Joelson, the economist at General Electric, was quoted in Louis Uchitelle, "Narrowing a Wage Gap," *New York Times*, June 26, 1987. The article was cited in Mattera, *Prosperity Lost* (see chap. 1, n. 17). Dr. Krause was participating with other academics from the University of California at San Diego in a briefing for congressional staff members investigating issues surrounding NAFTA, May 4, 1991.

4. U.S. Bureau of Labor Statistics, "International Comparisons of Hourly Compensation Costs for Production Workers in Manufacturing, 1975, 1980, and 1985-91, Supplementary Tables for BLS Report 825" (Washington, DC: Government Printing Office, June 1992). Including benefits and the employer's contribution to social security brings the average hourly figure in the United States to $15.45 per hour. Including these costs still leaves the United States in twelfth place, but shifts Japan to fourteenth. The international wage figures presented here should be considered rough guides rather than exact comparisons for two reasons. First, what one dollar will buy in Japan, for example, is quite different from what it will buy in the United States, so dollar-based comparisons are not the same as purchasing-power comparisons. This problem is exacerbated by wide swings in exchange rates. Second, countries engage in different industrial activities with different wage structures. A more accurate comparison would be among workers in the same industry in different countries.

5. Quoted in Louis Uchitelle, "As Output Gains, Wages Lag," *New York Times*, June 4, 1987. Cited in Mattera, *Prosperity Lost* (see chap. 1, n. 17).

6. This description is based on John P. Gaventa, "From the Mountains to the Maquiladoras: A Case Study of Capital Flight and Its Impact on Workers" (Paper prepared for a project on "The Changing Economy of the South," New Market, TN: Highlander Research and Education Center, n.d.).

7. Cited in Steve Fox, *Toxic Work: Women Workers at GTE Lenkurt* (Philadelphia: Temple University Press, 1991), p. 31. In the mid-1980s Fantus changed its name to P.H.H. Fantus after its acquisition by a business management consulting firm.

8. Roger W. Schmenner, *Making Business Location Decisions* (Englewood Cliffs, NJ: Prentice-Hall, 1982), p. 37 and Table 3-20.

9. See Dan La Botz, *Mask of Democracy: Labor Suppression in Mexico Today* (Boston: South End Press, 1992). For a history of Mexican labor through the austerity of the 1980s, see Kevin Middlebrook, "The Sounds of Silence: Organized Labour's Response to Economic Crisis in Mexico," *Journal of Latin American Studies* 21, no. 2 (1989), pp. 195-220; Dan La Botz, *The Crisis of Mexican Labor* (New York: Praeger, 1988); and Jerome I. Levinson, *Unrequited Toil: Denial of Labor Rights in Mexico and Implications for NAFTA* (New York: World Policy Institute, April 1993). For recent reporting on the difficulties facing independent labor activists in Mexico, see Mary E. Tong, "Maquiladora Workers Unite: Tijuana Labor Struggles Are Fight for Survival," *Worker Rights News*, Spring 1993.

10. For a brief history of Mexican unionism, see George Grayson, *The Mexican Labor Machine: Power, Politics and Patronage* (Washington, DC: Center for Strategic and International Studies, 1989). See also Kevin J. Middlebrook, ed., *Unions, Workers, and the State in Mexico* (San Diego, CA: Center for U.S.-Mexican Studies, 1991).

11. Gene Erb, "U.S. Plants in Mexico: Better Life at Low Wages," *Des Moines Register*, March 17, 1986.

12. The "Big Three" are General Motors, Ford, and Chrysler.

13. Richard Child Hill, "Economic Crisis and Political Response in the Motor City," in Larry Sawers and William K. Tabb, eds., *Sunbelt/Snowbelt: Urban Development and Regional Restructuring* (New York: Oxford University Press, 1984), p. 314.

14. Information about this complex is drawn largely from Harley Shaiken, *Mexico in the Global Economy: High Technology and Work Organization in Export Industries* (San Diego, CA: Center for U.S.-Mexican Studies, 1990). Shaiken does not identify Ford by name, but the geographical description of the location together with other details about the parent firm leave little doubt as to the plant's identity.

15. Mexico's attitude was largely shaped by the ruling political party's economic strategy, which depended heavily on foreign investment. Like most unions in Mexico, Ford's was formally part of the party structure and was constrained from challenging top political priorities.

16. Michael Satchell, "Poisoning the Border," *U.S. News and World Report*, May 6, 1991, p. 36.

17. The figures for the furniture and chemical industries are from David J. Molina, "A Comment on Whether Maquiladoras Are in Mexico for Low Wages or to Avoid Pollution Abatement Costs," *The Journal of Environment and Development* 2, no. 1 (Winter 1993).

18. Downtown City Television/NBC Investigative Reports, John Alpert, producer, 1987. Cited in Steve Fox, *Toxic Chemicals and Stress* (Ph.D. diss., University of New Mexico, 1988), p. 211.

19. Leslie Kochan, *Maquiladoras: The Hidden Cost of Production South of the Border* (Washington, DC: AFL-CIO, 1990). Kochan works with the Oregon Department of Environmental Quality.

20. Martin Eder, "Factory on the Run," *Fuera de Línea*, Summer 1992, pp. 13-15; Norma de la Vega Maciel, "Alerta contra la mudanza de una planta contaminadora a Tecate," *Proceso*, March 30, 1992, p. 44; and Andrew Cohen, "The Downside of 'Development,' " *The Nation*, Nov. 4, 1991, pp. 544-46.

21. From Jeannie Kever, "A Thousand Lives," *San Antonio Light*, Nov. 13, 1990.

22. Statement of the National Safe Workplace Institute in hearings before the U.S. Senate Committee on Finance, *United States-Mexico Free Trade Agreement*, 102d Cong., 1st sess., Feb. 6 and 20, 1991, p. 375.

23. Ibid., p. 374. Also see Rafael Moure-Eraso et al., "Back to the Future: Sweatshop Conditions of the Mexico-U.S. Border" (Final report, University of Lowell—Work Environment Program, May 21, 1991), and the studies of Catalina A. Denman, professor at the Colegio de Sonora, including "Tiempos Modernos: Trabajar y Morir" (Paper presented at a roundtable sponsored by the Friedrich Ebert Foundation, Hermosillo, Sonora, Nov. 6-7, 1989), and her masters' thesis, "Repercusiones de la industria maquiladora de exportación en la salud: El peso al nacer de hijos de obreras en Nogales" (Colegio de Sonora, 1988).

24. Joseph LaDou, "Deadly Migration," *Technology Review* (July 1991), p. 50.

25. Roberto A. Sánchez, "Environment: Mexican Perspective," in Sidney Weintraub, ed., *U.S.-Mexican Industrial Integration: The Road to Free Trade* (Boulder: Westview Press, 1991), p. 308.

26. Sections of this summary, including all quotes, are excerpted with the author's permission from Fox, *Toxic Work* (see chap. 2, n. 7).

27. As of 1986, only ninety of the 1,900 firms belonging to the American Electronics Association had unions representing their production workers. Kenneth Geiser, "Health Hazards of the Microelectronics Industry," *International Journal of Health Services* (Jan. 1986), pp. 105-15. Only 2.7 percent of electronics and computer equipment workers belonged to unions in the early 1990s. Elizabeth Kadetsky, "High-Tech's Dirty Little Secret," *The Nation*, April 19, 1993, pp. 517-20.

28. According to Lacy, GTE Lenkurt hired him away from the Occupational Safety and Health Administration to keep him from reporting 150 serious violations he had discovered.

29. GTE appeared to tip the odds against getting caught. One employee stated she found a co-worker extremely upset in a bathroom in the plant. "I said, 'My gosh, Irene, what's wrong?'. . . And she said, 'They're making me change all the labels on all those barrels out there because OSHA is coming to check.' "

30. GTE Lenkurt's plants in Albuquerque and Ciudad Juárez were sold in the mid-1980s to the German firm Siemens AG, making it very difficult to determine GTE's practices while it managed the Mexican plant.

31. Satchell, "Poisoning the Border" (see chap. 2, n. 16), p. 36. The Resource Conservation and Recovery Act requires "cradle-to-grave" reporting of the generation, transport, storage, and disposal of hazardous materials within the United States.

32. Sanford J. Lewis, Marco Kaltofen, and Mary Waygan, *Border Trouble: Rivers in Peril* (Boston: National Toxics Campaign Fund, May 1991).

33. International Labor Organization, *Safety and Health Practices of Multinational Enterprises* (Geneva, 1984), pp. 58-59. At the same time, however, Mexican authorities viewed the health and safety performance of the TNCs as being superior to those of domestically owned operations.

34. See John Maggs, "GM Agrees to Treat Water at 35 Maquiladora Plants," *Journal of Commerce*, May 15, 1991.

35. Sandy Tolan, "Hope and Heartbreak," *New York Times Magazine*, July 1, 1990.

36. Dick Kamp, "Lime Dust in My Children's Lungs," Testimony before the EPA, Sept. 26, 1991, Nogales, Arizona.

37. Molina, "A Comment" (see chap. 2, n. 17).

38. Satchell, "Poisoning the Border" (see chap. 2, n. 16), p. 41.

39. Alejandro Mercado, José Negrete, and Roberto Sánchez, *Capital internacional y relocalización industrial en la Frontera Norte de México* (Tijuana: COLEF, 1989).

40. See Gene M. Grossman and Alan B. Krueger, "Environmental Impacts of a North American Free Trade Agreement," discussion paper no. 158 (Princeton, NJ: Woodrow Wilson School of Government, Princeton University, Feb. 1992); Stephen P. Mumme, "Complex Interdependence and Hazardous Waste Management along the U.S.-Mexico Border," in Charles E. Davis and James P. Lester, eds., *Dimensions of Hazardous Waste Politics and Policy* (New York: Greenwood Press, 1988); H. Jeffrey Leonard, *Are Environmental Regulations Driving U.S. Industry Overseas?* (Washington, DC: The Conservation Foundation, 1984); Christopher Duerksen and H. Jeffrey Leonard, "Environmental Regulations and the Location of Industries: An International Perspective," *Columbia Journal of World Business* (Summer 1982); and Barry Castleman, "How We Export Dangerous Industries," *Business and Society Review* (Fall 1978).

41. Much of the information in this summary is from Judy Pasternak, "Firms Find a Haven From U.S. Environmental Rules," *Los Angeles Times*, Nov. 19, 1991.

42. Cited in LaDou, "Deadly Migration" (see chap. 2, n. 24), p. 50.

Chapter 3

1. Ford invested $300 million in Hermosillo and $700 million in Chihuahua.

2. Portuguese welfare would improve in this case, at least under Ricardo's model, which postulated full employment, and it could be argued that, under the same full employment assumption, global welfare had also increased. But the key feature of comparative advantage—that *all* trading partners benefit from open trade—no longer holds.

3. An expansive literature has developed on this subject over the last fifteen years. One of the best works is Michael J. Piore and Charles F. Sabel, *The Second Industrial Divide: Possibilities for Prosperity* (New York: Basic Books, 1984). See also Michael L. Dertouzos, Richard K. Lester, and Robert M. Solow, *Made in America: Regaining the Productive Edge* (New York: HarperPerennial, 1989), and Robert R. Reich, *The Next American Frontier* (New York: Times Books, 1983). There are a few documented cases of trend-bucking plants moving from low-wage areas back to the United States (see Susan Sanderson, "American Industry Can Go Home Again," *Across the Board* 23, no. 2 [Feb. 1986]), but no large-scale movement is occurring.

4. See, for example: Patricia Wilson, "The New Maquiladoras: Flexible Production in Low Wage Regions," in Khosrow Fatemi, ed., *Maquiladoras: Economic Problem or Solution?* (New York: Praeger, 1990); Piore and Sabel, *The Second Industrial Divide*, ibid.; D. Barnett and Robert Crandall, *Up from the Ashes: The Rise of the Steel Minimill in the United States* (Washington, DC: Brookings, 1986); and James Womack, Daniel Jones, and Daniel Roos, *The Machine that Changed the World* (New York: Rawson Associates, 1990).

5. Works on management's quest for work-force flexibility and control—from both approving and critical viewpoints—include Thomas Kochan, Harry Katz, and Robert McKersie, *The Transformation of American Industrial Relations* (New York: Basic Books, 1986); Harley

Shaiken, *Work Transformed* (Lexington, MA: Lexington Books, 1986); Mike Parker and Jane Slaughter, "Management by Stress," *Technology Review* (Oct. 1988), pp. 37-44; and Robert Howard, *Brave New Workplace* (New York: Simon and Schuster, 1985).

6. Aaron Bernstein, "The Global Economy: Who Gets Hurt," *Business Week*, Aug. 10, 1992, p. 52.

Chapter 4

1. Unfortunately, this review of possible strategies and tactics will have to be brief. Given the size of this book and the immensity of the task, the discussion will necessarily be limited to just a few of the most helpful signposts on the roads that seem most likely to get us from here—economic decline and political weakness—to there—sustainable, equitable, and democratic economic development. Those signposts have been drawn up by unionists, community activists, economists, and scholars who have wrestled with these issues for years. The people and organizations who have contributed to the ideas discussed in the following pages are too many to mention here. Throughout the discussion, however, their works will be footnoted and their organizations named wherever possible. In addition, the list of publications and organizations given in Appendix C includes many excellent sources of information and assistance.

2. Strategies for building strong grassroots coalitions—both national and transnational—are explored in the following works: Jeremy Brecher and Tim Costello, eds., *Building Bridges: The Emerging Grassroots Coalition of Labor and Community* (New York: Monthly Review Press, 1990), and Peter Rachleff, *Hard-Pressed in the Heartland: The Hormel Strike and the Future of the Labor Movement* (Boston: South End Press, 1993).

3. See Kim Moody, *An Injury to All* (see chap. 1, n. 11).

4. A number of authors have criticized the U.S. labor federation and its international institutes for their activities abroad. These include: Sims, *Workers of the World Undermined* (see chap. 1, n. 11); Ronald Radosh, *American Labor and United States Foreign Policy* (New York: Random House, 1969); and Cantor and Schor, *Tunnel Vision* (see chap. 1, n. 1).

5. See especially Brecher and Costello, *Building Bridges* (see chap. 4, n. 2).

6. For overviews of a number of these approaches, see Greg LeRoy, Dan Swinney, and Elaine Charpentier, *Early Warning Manual Against Plant Closings* (Chicago: Midwest Center for Labor Research, 1988), pp. 81-93; *Industrial Retention: Proven Local and State-Level Initiatives* (Chicago: Midwest Center for Labor Research, Feb. 1991); and the entire issue of *Labor Research Review*, no. 19 (Fall 1992).

7. For a brief look at these responses, see *Industrial Retention*, ibid.

8. The problem of undemocratic and bureaucratized unionism is especially acute at the level of the national and international union bodies. For a compelling first-hand account of the lack of support from the United Food and Commercial Workers (UFCW) for militant labor actions at its P-9 local during the Hormel strike in Austin, Minnesota, see Rachleff, *Hard-Pressed in the Heartland* (see chap. 4, n. 2).

9. This is not a suggestion that government should jump in and bail out big business while hanging the workers and the community out to dry. Our recommendation is that, if there is government intervention in the forms of grants, low-cost loans, or other special financing, there be strings attached requiring various commitments on the part of the corporation in such areas as investments, new product lines, and duration of operations. Better still, the terms of the company's commitment to the community as a result of government support might be worked out democratically, with input from workers and other members of the community.

10. *Plant Closings: Limited Advance Notice and Assistance Provided Dislocated Workers* (Washington, DC: General Accounting Office, 1987).

11. For a complete list of early-warning indicators, see LeRoy et al., *Early Warning Manual* (see chap. 4, n. 6), pp. 13-36.

12. Interview with Karen May, Midwest Center for Labor Research, May 25, 1993.

13. LeRoy et al., *Early Warning Manual* (see chap. 4, n. 6), pp. 39-43.

14. A good description of the campaign to save LaSalle Steel is given in Bruce Nissen and Lynn Feekin, "For the Public Good," *Labor Research Review*, no. 19 (Fall 1992).

15. Written comments by Feekin in response to research questions from the Resource Center, March 25, 1993.

16. LeRoy et al., *Early Warning Manual* (see chap. 4, n. 6), p. 19.

17. For a blow-by-blow description of unsuccessful efforts by displaced workers and their community coalition partners to buy and operate steel facilities in Youngstown, Ohio, during the late 1970s and early 1980s, see the informative work by Staughton Lynd, a participant in the effort. Lynd, *The Fight Against Shutdowns* (see chap. 1, n. 11).

18. For a complete overview of worker ownership, including a discussion of the fundamentals of workplace democracy and how to organize a business so that it is viable economically, see Frank T. Adams and Gary B. Hansen, *Putting Democracy to Work: A Practical Guide for Starting and Managing Worker-Owned Businesses* (San Francisco: Berrett-Koehler Publishers, 1992).

19. This assessment comes from the Calumet Project for Industrial Jobs, a nonprofit organization dedicated to job retention and economic development in northwest Indiana. The Calumet Project also found that Indiana communities were not getting what they paid for with their subsidies. In Hammond, Indiana, during 1989 alone, more than $15 million in abatements had been granted to sixteen companies. Some 804 jobs had been promised by the companies in exchange for this support, but only seventy-four jobs were actually created. Nissen and Feekin, "For the Public Good" (see chap. 4, n. 14), p. 21.

20. See *Industrial Retention* (see chap. 4, n. 6), pp. 7-8.

21. Janet Koch, "City Runaway Law May Affect New Aid Pacts," *New Haven Register*, Dec. 20, 1985.

22. Nissen and Feekin, "For the Public Good" (see chap. 4, n. 14), p. 23.

23. The success of this approach is also limited by the fact that corporate promises are often made orally but are not captured in the language of the contract. To protect the community—and provide the best case should the matter reach the courts—city and state governments must include the specific terms of the agreement in contracts, and require penalties for misrepresentations or falsehoods on subsidy applications and for violations of the contract.

24. For background on the case, see LeRoy et al., *Early Warning Manual* (see chap. 4, n. 6), pp. 54-57.

25. This following discussion is based largely on *Industrial Retention* (see chap. 4, n. 6).

26. On the Steel Valley Authority, see Jim Benn, "Industrial Policy Blues," *CrossRoads*, no. 22 (Sept. 1992), and Tom Croft, "Achieving City Pride," *Labor Research Review*, no. 19 (Fall 1992).

27. For more on the following discussion, see *Industrial Retention* (see chap. 4, n. 6).

28. The Federation for Industrial Retention and Renewal has compiled a number of recommendations for a new WARN Act, including the above suggestions and other requirements such as mandating that the company open its books in addition to paying severance, health care, and training costs of displaced workers. See Julie Hurwitz, "Why We Need a Better WARN Act," *FIRR Notes*, Jan. 1993, and Roger Kerson and Greg LeRoy, *State and Local Initiatives on Development Subsidies and Plant Closings* (Chicago: Federation for Industrial Retention and Renewal, 1989).

29. For a look at the strong and weak points of EDWAA, see Greg LeRoy, "WARN and EDWAA: Use 'em or Lose 'em," *Labor Research Review*, no. 19 (Fall 1992).

30. Statement of the Tri-State Conference on Steel, cited in Rachael Kamel, *The Global Factory: Analysis and Action for a New Economic Era* (Philadelphia: American Friends Service Committee, 1990), p. 34.

31. A critique of "conservative," "liberal," "corporatist," and other common strategies for industrial development is given in Bluestone and Harrison, *The Deindustrialization of America* (see chap. 1, n. 5), pp 193-230. The article explores options for "reindustrialization with a hu-

man face." Proposals include a strengthened social safety net, adequate plant-closing leg-islation, public support for alternative forms of ownership, expanded public support for social goods like health care and housing, and targeted public investment balanced by at least minority public ownership of the assisted firms. The authors also call for movement toward a more "radical" industrial policy based on the fundamental values of equity and democracy. See pp. 231-64.

32. Bowles et al., *After the Waste Land* (see chap. 1, n. 1), p. 203.

33. Ibid. The Federation for Industrial Retention and Renewal is also making an effort to sketch the outlines of a national industrial policy. "Toward FIRR's Industrial Policy" (Chicago: Federation for Industrial Retention and Renewal, n.d.).

34. In a 1990 interview, Jim Hightower, a populist who served as commissioner of agriculture in Texas, discussed some of the ways that government can promote alternative forms of ownership, workplace democracy, and economic development while working within a market structure. "Bringing Back Populism," *Dollars & Sense*, Jan.-Feb. 1990.

35. See: Brecher and Costello, *Building Bridges* (see chap. 4, n. 2); Jeremy Brecher and Tim Costello, *Global Village vs. Global Pillage: A One-World Strategy for Labor* (Washington, DC: International Labor Rights Education and Research Fund, 1991); Jeremy Brecher, "The Stupid Economy," *Z Magazine*, April 1993; and Jeremy Brecher, "International Capital Mobility and the U.S. Economy," *Z Papers*, n.d.

36. Brecher and Costello, *Global Village vs. Global Pillage*, ibid., pp. 1-2.

37. Ibid., p. 3.

38. *Environmental, Religious and Labor Organizations Promote Corporate Social Responsibility in the Maquiladora Industry* (San Antonio, TX: Coalition for Justice in the Maquiladoras, n.d.).

39. Comments on the draft of *Runaway America*. April 7, 1993.

40. For overviews of these laws and U.S. obligations under them, see: *Human Rights and U.S. Foreign Policy: Worker Rights under the U.S. Trade Laws* (New York: Lawyers Committee for Human Rights, 1989); Richard Rothstein, *Setting the Standard: International Labor Rights and U.S. Trade Policy*, briefing paper (Washington, DC: Economic Policy Institute, March 1993); and Jorge F. Perez-Lopez, "Worker Rights in the U.S. Omnibus Trade and Competitiveness Act," *Labor Law Journal* (April 1990).

41. The rights in question are: the right of association, the right to organize and bargain collectively, prohibitions on the use of forced labor, a minimum age for the employment of children, and acceptable conditions of work in terms of minimum wages, hours of work, and occupational health and safety.

42. See the discussion in Stephen A. Herzenberg, *Institutionalizing Constructive Competition: International Labor Standards and Trade, Economic Discussion Paper 32* (Washington, DC: Office of International Economic Affairs, U.S. Department of Labor, Sept. 1988), pp. 16-18.

43. Peter Dorman, "The Social Tariff Approach to International Disparities in Environmental and Worker Rights Standards: History, Theory, and Some Initial Evidence" (Unpublished paper, University of California-Riverside, Nov. 1987). Cited in ibid, p. 17.

44. Inspired by concerns about NAFTA, coalitions of environmentalists, labor organizations, religious groups, and community activists in the United States and Mexico have drawn the broad outlines of a pro-people and pro-environment framework for economic integration. Organizations such as the Alliance for Responsible Trade, Citizen Trade Watch Campaign, Coalition for Justice in the Maquiladoras, Fair Trade Campaign, Action Canada Network, and Mexican Action Network on Free Trade have been among the most active. Most of the following discussion about ways to shape integration draws on the important work of groups like these and the publications of analysts and activists who share their concerns. See, for example, George E. Brown Jr., J. William Goold, and John Cavanagh, "Making Trade Fair," *World Policy Journal* (Spring 1992); Gregory, "Environment, Sustainable Development, Public Participation" (see chap. 1, n. 2); Andrew A. Reding, "Bolstering Democracy in the Americas," *World Policy Journal* (Summer 1992); and Cuauhtémoc Cárdenas, "The Continental Development and Trade Initiative" (Speech given before the Americas Society, New York, Feb. 8, 1991). For a directory of organizations conducting transboundary activities, see Ricardo Hernández and Edith Sánchez, eds., *Cross-Border Links: A Directory of*

Organizations in Canada, Mexico, and the United States (Albuquerque, NM: Inter-Hemispheric Education Resource Center, 1992).

45. A number of authors have criticized the economic and trade policy process for its undemocratic nature. For two of the most detailed examinations, see Gregory, "Environment, Sustainable Development, Public Participation" (see chap. 1, n. 2); and Mead, "Bushism, Found" (see chap. 1, n. 2). Also see Noam Chomsky, "The Masters of Mankind," *The Nation*, March 29, 1993.

46. Three pro-NAFTA economists suggested that a North American Development Bank and Adjustment Fund (NADBAF) be set up to finance the development and adjustment costs of NAFTA. Albert Fishlow, Sherman Robinson, and Raul Hinojosa-Ojeda, "Proposal for a North American Regional Development Bank and Adjustment Fund" (Presented at a conference on North American Free Trade sponsored by the Federal Reserve Bank of Dallas, Dallas, Texas, June 14, 1991). See also U.S. Congress, Office of Technology Assessment, *U.S.-Mexico Trade: Pulling Together or Pulling Apart?* (Washington, DC: Government Printing Office, Oct. 1992), p. 52. Critics have pointed out that, without adequate controls, financing such as that recommended by Fishlow et al. could simply subsidize corporate flight (by building infrastructure, for example, or by helping to clean up pollution that businesses themselves should pay for, for example). A first step toward an alternative proposal for a development bank that would address the grassroots needs of the NAFTA countries was advanced by Nikos Valance of the Fair Trade Campaign. See his memorandum on the NAFTA Development Bank (New York: Fair Trade Campaign, July 14, 1992)

47. Thea Lee, an analyst at the Economic Policy Institute, recommended that such aid not be channeled through banks, Mexico's ruling party, or U.S. transnational corporations, but that it be designated for development and adjustment assistance controlled by communities, workers, and their representatives.

48. See the discussion of such programs in Tom Barry, Harry Browne, and Beth Sims, *The Great Divide: The Challenge of U.S.-Mexico Relations in the 1990s* (New York: Grove/Atlantic, forthcoming).

49. The basic components of a code of conduct for transnational corporations, are described in Brecher and Costello, *Global Village vs. Global Pillage* (see chap. 4, n. 35). In a major setback to efforts to install such a code, an intergovernmental group at the United Nations declared in late 1992 that no consensus was possible on provisions of the code. The group's conclusions marked the end of a thirteen-year process to create and install the code under United Nations auspices.

50. See Herzenberg, *Institutionalizing Constructive Competition* (see chap. 4, n. 42), and Rothstein, *Setting the Standard* (see chap. 4, n. 40).

51. Among the many authors or organizations that have explored the idea of a social charter that would parallel or be contained within a free trade agreement are: U.S. Congress, Office of Technology Assessment, *U.S.-Mexico Trade* (see chap. 4, n. 46), pp. 48-50; Brown et al., "Making Trade Fair" (see chap. 4, n. 44); Seminario Permanente de Estudios Chicanos y de Fronteras, "Proposal for a Tri-National Declaration of Human Rights" (Mexico City, 1992); J.M. Servais, "The Social Clause in Trade Agreements: Wishful Thinking or an Instrument of Social Progress?" *International Labour Review* 128, no. 4 (1989); Gijsbert van Liemt, "Minimum Labour Standards and International Trade: Would a Social Clause Work?" *International Labour Review* 128, no. 4 (1989); and Matthew Sanger, "Free Trade and Workers' Rights: The European Social Charter," *Briarpatch* (Saskatchewan) 20, no. 7 (Sept. 1991).

The Runaways

The following list summarizes fifteen months of research into the relocation of jobs from the United States to Mexico. The methodology we used to compile the list is described in Appendix B.

We have attempted to include the most relevant information about each runaway, including the names of parent companies and of the subsidiaries in the United States and Mexico that were involved in the transfer of work. The name of the Mexican subsidiary was not always available, in which cases that entry was left blank. "Jobs Lost" refers only to jobs directly transferred to Mexico; in many cases the figure is only a fraction of the total number of workers laid off at a given work site. A "⇐" in the Jobs Lost column indicates that the company decided to shift work back to the United States from Mexico several years after sending it abroad. "Type" indicates whether a plant was closed ("C") entirely or whether a portion of the plant's production was moved ("M") to Mexico. A blank entry in this column indicates that the information was unavailable. In other columns, "n/a" is used to indicate unavailable information.

They can run.
But they cannot hide.

Help us expose them!

Tracking runaways is an ongoing project. If you have information relating to the direct shipment of jobs from the United States to low-wage countries, please let us know about it. Any details concerning the company, the number of jobs, the product line or lines, the date, or the destination would be appreciated, as would any related press clippings or other materials.

Send to:

Resource Center
c/o Runaways Project
Box 4506
Albuquerque, NM 87196
(505) 842-8288
Fax: (505) 246-1601

Please include your name, address, and phone number, and indicate your source(s) of information about the runaway jobs.

Thanks for your help!

T H E   R U N A W A Y S

From the United States . . . to Mexico

PARENT COMPANY	SUBSIDIARY	LOCATION	PRODUCT	JOBS LOST	TIME SPAN	TYPE	MEXICO COMPANY	MEXICO LOCATION
Allied-Signal	Bendix Safety Restraints	Greensville, AL	Seat belts	500	1986-90	M	American Safety Bendix, Sistemas Seguridad Bendix	Agua Prieta (2 plants), Cd. Juárez
Goldstar (South Korea)	Goldstar America	Huntsville, AL	TV assembly	200	1988 & 1992	C	Electra Estrella de Oro	Mexicali
Munsingwear	Vassarette	Guin & Hamilton, AL	Women's undergarments	ca. 250	1989	C	Rey Mex Bra	Reynosa
National Industries		Union Springs, AL	Wire harnesses for autos	371	1991	C		Empalme, 2 others
National Industries		Montgomery & Werumpka, AL	Wire harnesses for autos	475	1991	M		Empalme, 2 others
AT&T		Little Rock, AR	Telephone answering machines	470	1989	C	AT&T Productos de Consumo México	Guadalajara
Chamberlain Group		Jones Mill, AR	Aluminum door manufacturing (not garage doors)	130+ ⟸	1990	M	Grupo Chamberlain	Nogales
MagneTek		Blytheville, AR	Fluorescent ballasts	600	1988	M	MagneTek Matamoros	Matamoros
MagneTek	Universal Manufacturing	Jonesboro, AR	Light ballasts	600	1988-89	M	MagneTek Matamoros	Matamoros
Sanyo Manufacturing (Japan)		Forrest City, AR	13" & 20" TVs & microwaves	1400	1986-87	M		Matamoros
Chrysler	Coleman Products	Nogales, AZ	Wiring leads for harnesses	250	1988-89	C	Coleman de Obregón	Cd. Obregón
Emerson Electric	U.S. Motors	Prescott, AZ	Motors	270	1986-87	C	Motores U.S. de México	Apodaca, Cd. Juárez

THE RUNAWAYS

From the United States... to Mexico

PARENT COMPANY	SUBSIDIARY	LOCATION	PRODUCT	JOBS LOST	TIME SPAN	TYPE	MEXICO COMPANY	MEXICO LOCATION
Motorola		Phoenix, AZ	Semiconductors	900	1985	M	Motorola de México	Guadalajara
Artis		Buellton, CA	Arts & crafts materials	52	1991	M		Tijuana
Bayly		Sanger, CA	Apparel (OP, Bugle Boy)	ca. 350	1990	C	Bayly Mexicana	Allende, Coahuila
Bayly		Visalia, CA	Apparel (OP, Bugle Boy)	ca. 250	1988	C	Bayly Mexicana	Allende, Coahuila
Cardinal Tables of California		Chatsworth, CA	Furniture	130	1990	C		Tijuana
Carlisle Plastics		Santa Ana, CA	Plastic clothes hangers	n/a	1990	M	Plásticos Baja	Tijuana
CFR International		San Diego, CA	Antennae	ca. 250	1990	C		Tijuana, Ensenada, Mexico City, Coahuila
Cohart Products		Los Angeles, CA	Pipe fixtures	n/a	1987-90			Tijuana
Cooper Industries	Halo Lighting	Los Angeles, CA	Lighting fixtures	100	1988	M	Componentes de Illuminación	Cd. Juárez
Cooper Industries	Wagner Brake	Los Angeles, CA	Brake shoes	115	1991	C		Tijuana
Cubic	U.S. Elevator	Spring Valley, CA	Elevators & parts	ca. 100	1985-89	C		Mexicali (2 plants)
Douglas Furniture		Los Angeles, CA	Dining room furniture & recliners	n/a	1985	M	Industrias Cokin	Tijuana

THE RUNAWAYS

From the United States . . .   *to Mexico*

PARENT COMPANY	SUBSIDIARY	LOCATION	PRODUCT	JOBS LOST	TIME SPAN	TYPE	MEXICO COMPANY	MEXICO LOCATION
Eastman Kodak (now Mitsubishi)	Verbatim	Sunnyvale, CA		up to 400	1986	C	Kayamex, Fleximedia de México	Tijuana, Nogales
Eric Morgan		Vernon, CA	Furniture	ca. 200	1989	C		Tijuana
Finegood Furniture	Good Bedrooms	Carson & Compton, CA	Furniture	600	1990-91	C	Muebles Fino Bueno	Tijuana
Fisher Scientific Group	Imed Group	Los Angeles, CA	Tubing, valves for medical pumps	Dozens	1988	M		Tijuana
General Dynamics	Electronics Div.	San Diego, CA	Cables & harnesses for military testing	100	1989	M	Calitec	Tijuana
General Electric		Oakland, CA	Wire/cable	300	1983	C	Productos de Control	Nogales
Genisco Technology	Genisco Electronics	La Mirada, CA	Surge protectors	50	1990	C		Tijuana
Grand Metropolitan (UK)	Pillsbury/Green Giant	Watsonville, CA	Broccoli & cauliflower processing	670	1983 & 1991	M	Gigante Verde	Irapuato
GTE	GTE Lenkurt	Redwood City, CA	Coil transformers	500	1984	M		Cd. Juárez
GTE-Valeron	Valenite	Riverside, CA	Machine tools	n/a	Early 1980s	C		Mexicali
Hitachi America Ltd. (Japan)	Hitachi Consumer Products	Anaheim, CA	Televisions, TV cabinets	250	1992	C	Hitachi Consumer Products de México	Tijuana

THE RUNAWAYS

From the United States . . . to Mexico

PARENT COMPANY	SUBSIDIARY	LOCATION	PRODUCT	JOBS LOST	TIME SPAN	TYPE	MEXICO COMPANY	MEXICO LOCATION
Honeywell	Residential Controls Div.	Gardena, CA	Heating/air-condtioning thermostats	500	1988-91	M	Mexhon	Tijuana
Hyundai Motor (South Korea)		Long Beach, CA	Shipboard containers	300	1989	C		Tijuana
Kransco Group		San Gabriel, CA	Hula hoops, frisbees, toys	ca. 200	1985-87	M	Juegos California	Tijuana
Lancer Orthodontics		Carlsbad, CA	Orthodontics	90	1991	C		Mexicali
LeVone Manufacturing		Los Angeles, CA	Laminated wood & upholstered products	70	1992	C	Muebles LeVon	Tijuana
Louisiana-Pacific		Covelo, Potter Valley, & Cloverdale, CA	Redwood planing & fenceboards	100	1989-91	C		El Sauzal (Ensenada)
Mattel		Paramount, CA	Toys	250	1987-88	C	Mabamex (2 plants), Montoi	Tijuana, Tecate, Sta. Catalina
Mattel		Covina, CA	Plastic toy assembly	800	1986-90	C	Mabamex (2 plants), Montoi	Tijuana, Tecate, Sta. Catalina
Mr. Gasket		Los Angeles, CA	Mufflers/exhaust systems	n/a	1986	M	Fabricaciones Metálicas Mexicanas	Mexicali
Nellcor		Hayward, CA	Medical equipment	370	1989-90	C	Nellcor de México	Tijuana
Northern Telecom		Santa Clara, CA	Telephone handsets	230	1993	M		Monterrey

THE RUNAWAYS

From the United States . . .

to Mexico

PARENT COMPANY	SUBSIDIARY	LOCATION	PRODUCT	JOBS LOST	TIME SPAN	TYPE	MEXICO COMPANY	MEXICO LOCATION
Ocean Pacific		Los Angeles, CA	Ladies swimsuits	n/a	1987	M	Creaciones Donaji	Tecate
Outdoor Technology Group	Fenwick	Westminster, CA	Fishing rods	n/a	1989	C	Outdoor Technology International	Merida
Philips Industries NV	Philips Components	Los Angeles, CA	Multilayer ceramic chip capacitors	n/a	1991	C	Centalab	Cd. Juárez
Rockwell International		Santa Ana, CA	Semiconductors	40	1985	M	Autonética	Mexicali
Sandberg Furniture Manufacturing		Vernon, CA	Furniture	n/a	1991	C		Tijuana
Sanyo Industries (America)		San Diego, CA	Small refrigerators	n/a	1983	M	SIA Electrónica	Tijuana
Sun-Diamond Growers	Diamond Walnut Growers	Stockton, CA	Walnut processing	100	1985	M	Productos del Valle Grande	Tijuana
Taiyo Yuden (Japan)	Xentek	Vista, CA	Transformers & power supplies	130	1992	C		Tijuana
Vargas Furniture		Los Angeles, CA	Furniture	n/a	Late 1980s			Tijuana
Wood Textures		Tustin, CA	Tables, chairs, & entertainment centers	200	1989-90	M		Tecate
ACS Industries	Adirondack Wire & Cable	Torrington, CT	Telephone cords	n/a	1988	C	ACS Internacional	Monterrey
Airshield		Bridgeport, CT	Aerodynamic Shields	40	1991	M		Matamoros

T H E   R U N A W A Y S

From the United States . . . to Mexico

PARENT COMPANY	SUBSIDIARY	LOCATION	PRODUCT	JOBS LOST	TIME SPAN	TYPE	MEXICO COMPANY	MEXICO LOCATION
BTR PLC (UK)	Stewart-Warner Bassick Div.	Bridgeport, CT	Casters for furniture & equipment	ca. 200	1989-91	C	Industrias Hage	Cd. Juárez
Circuit Wise		New Haven, CT	Wire harnesses for autos	46	1992	M	Circuitos Impresos de Chihuahua	Chihuahua
Cooper Industries	Arrow Hart	Danielson, CT	Electric components & switches	200	1986	C	Arrow Hart & Componentes e Interruptores	Guadalajara & Cd. Juárez
Cooper Industries	Bussman Div.	Bristol, CT	Electric fuses	400	1991	C	Componentes e Interruptores	Cd. Juárez
LPL Technologies	Amphenol Products	Danbury, CT	Electrical connectors	140	1990 & 1992	M	Productos de Memoria	Nogales
Quality Coils		Stonington, CT	Electromagnetic coils	40 ⇐	1989	C		Cd. Juarez
William Prym		Dayville, CT	Sewing notions	106	1990		William Prym de México	Tulitlán, Edo. Mex.
Emerson Electric	Electronics & Space (ESCO)	Sanford, FL	Wiring for defense electronics	50	1989	M	Electronica y Espacio (ESMEX)	Cd. Juárez
Gates	Gates Energy	Gainesville, FL	Rechargeable batteries	200	1980s		Sistemas de Baterías	Cd. Juárez
Saft America		Valdosta, GA	Batteries	85	1989-92	M	Componentes Técnicos de B.C.	Tijuana
A.C. Nielsen (Dun & Bradstreet)	Nielsen Clearing House	Clinton, IA	Coupon sorting	100+	1966-86	M		Cd. Juárez, Delicias, Chihuahua, Cuauhtémoc, Nuevo Laredo
Kast Metals		Keokuk, IA	Cast metal products	n/a	1987	C	Fundidora de Metales del Bravo	Cd. Camargo
Wells Manufacturing		Manning, IA	Automobile ignitions	100+	1988-89	C	Wells Manufacturera de México	Reynosa

THE RUNAWAYS

From the United States . . . to Mexico

PARENT COMPANY	SUBSIDIARY	LOCATION	PRODUCT	JOBS LOST	TIME SPAN	TYPE	MEXICO COMPANY	MEXICO LOCATION
Zenith Electronics		Sioux City, IA	Consumer electronics	1500+	1978	C	Partes de Televisión de Reynosa	Reynosa
A.O. Smith		Kankakee, IL	Water heaters/ boilers for heating	310	1988	C	Productos de Agua	Cd. Juárez
BRK Electronics	Pittway	Chicago, IL	Smoke detectors	400	1989-92		Electrónica BRK de México	Cd. Juárez
BTR PLC (UK)	Stewart-Warner	Chicago, IL	Instrument gauges for heavy vehicles	ca. 700	1989-91	C	Industrias Hage	Cd. Juárez
BTR PLC (UK)	Stewart-Warner	Spring Valley, IL	Auto instrumentation (speedometers)	up to 1000	1989-91	C	Industrias Hage	Cd. Juárez
Cooper Industries	Crouse-Hinds	Chicago, IL	Outdoor light equipment	90	1985	M	Componentes de Iluminación	Cd. Juárez
Cooper Industries	Halo Lighting	Chicago, IL	Lighting fixtures	120	1990-91	M	Componentes de Iluminación	Cd. Juárez
Eureka Manufacturing		Bloomington, IL	Vacuum assembly & components	200+	1980s-1990s	M	Appliance Componentes	Cd. Juárez
Lamkin Leather & Rubber		Chicago, IL	Rubber products.	240		C	Lamkin de México	Tijuana
LPL Technologies/Amphenol	Pyle National	Chicago, IL	Electric connectors for aviation	n/a	1992	M	Productos de Memoria	Nogales
Mallinckrodt Medical		New Athens, IL	Temperature monitoring systems	75	1993	C		Undecided by company
Modern Filters		Joliet, IL	Fabric dust bags & filters	175	1985	C	Filtros Modernos de México	Cd. Juárez
Moog Automotive	Everco Div.	Skokie, IL	Auto parts	25	1989	C	Everco #1 & #2	Cd. Juárez

T H E   R U N A W A Y S

From the United States . . . to Mexico

PARENT COMPANY	SUBSIDIARY	LOCATION	PRODUCT	JOBS LOST	TIME SPAN	TYPE	MEXICO COMPANY	MEXICO LOCATION
Outboard Marine		Galesburg, IL	Outboard motors	up to 350	1983	C	Outboard Marine de México	Cd. Juárez
Philips Industries NV (Holland)	Advance Transformer	Chicago, IL	Ballasts/transformers	220-300	1989-90		Advance Transformer de México	Cd. Juárez
Paloma (Japan)	Rheem Manufacturing	Chicago, IL	Water heaters	518	1990	C	Industrias Rheem	Nuevo Laredo
Valmont Industries		Danville, IL	Light ballasts	90	1992	M	CCC de México	Cd. Juárez
Zenith Electronics		Paris, IL	TV parts	600	1983	C		Reynosa (2 plants), Cd. Juárez, Matamoros
Zenith Electronics		Chicago, IL	Cable TV decoders	300	1984	C	Cable Productos de Chihuahua	Chihuahua
Chrysler		Indianapolis, IN	Electric automotive parts	975	1988	C	Several plants	Cd. Juárez, others
Ford Motor	Ford Electronics & Refrigeration	Connersville, IN	Copper/brass radiators, hoses	450	1984 & 1993	M	Coclisa	Cd. Juárez
General Electric		Linton, IN	Wire winding & switch assembly	55		M		Cd. Juárez, Reynosa
General Electric		Tell City, IN	Small electric motors & parts	160	1985	M	Sociedad de Motores	Reynosa
General Electric	GE Motor Div.	Decatur, IN	Electric motors	500	1987-89	C		Cd. Juárez
General Motors	Delco Electronics	Kokomo, IN	Car radios	1300	1988-93	C	Delnosa	Reynosa, Matamoros (4 plants each)
Johnson Controls		Goshen, IN	Electric controls	300	1984-91		Controles Juarez & Controles Reynosa	Cd. Juárez, Reynosa

THE RUNAWAYS

From the United States . . . to Mexico

PARENT COMPANY	SUBSIDIARY	LOCATION	PRODUCT	JOBS LOST	TIME SPAN	TYPE	MEXICO COMPANY	MEXICO LOCATION
Phelps Dodge	Phelps Dodge Magnet Wire	Fort Wayne, IN	Fine magnet wire	30	1988	M		Cd. Juárez
Siemens AG (Germany)	Potter & Brumfield	Princeton, IN	Automotive relays	ca. 150	1992	M	Potter & Brumfield de México	Nuevo Casas Grandes, Cd. Juárez
Thomson Consumer Electronics (France)		Bloomington, IN	20" TVs	355	1991 & 1993	M	Thomson RCA Componentes & Productos Electrónicos de la Laguna	Cd. Juárez, Torreón
Thomson Consumer Electronics (France)		Indianapolis, IN	TV parts	2000+	1980-88		Thomson RCA Componentes & Productos Electrónicos de la Laguna	Cd. Juárez, Torreón
United Technologies	Otis Elevator	Bloomington, IN	Elevator control wiring	30	1990	M		Nogales
United Technologies	Essex Wire	Lafayette, IN	Wire harnesses for autos	184	1979	C	Essex Internacional	Cd. Juárez, Chihuahua
United Technologies	United Technologies Automotive	Wabash, IN	Wire cutting for wire harnesses	550	1987-91	C	Essex Internacional	Cd. Juárez
Zenith Electronics		Evansville, IN (2 plants)	Cabinets for TVs & consoles	1400	1986	C	Zenco	Cd. Juárez
A.O. Smith		Mt. Sterling, KY	Electric motors	ca. 1000	1980-92	M	10 electric motor/parts plants	Cd. Juárez & Cd. Acuña
Jason	Osborne Brush	Henderson, KY	Steel wire brushes	33	1992	C	Osborne de México	Nogales
Square D		Lexington, KY	Switch boxes	120	1990	M	Square D de México	Guadalajara

T H E   R U N A W A Y S

From the United States . . . to Mexico

PARENT COMPANY	SUBSIDIARY	LOCATION	PRODUCT	JOBS LOST	TIME SPAN	TYPE	MEXICO COMPANY	MEXICO LOCATION
AT&T		Shreveport, LA	Telephone sets (manufacturing)	100	1991-92	M		Monterrey
Digital Equipment		Westfield, MA	Microcomputers, cables & harnesses	100	1986	M		Chihuahua
Foster Grant		Leominster, MA	Low-end sunglasses	340	1986	M	Foster Grant de México	Nogales
General Electric		Pittsfield, MA	Transformers	100+	1986	M	Productos de Control	Cd. Juárez
General Electric		Pittsfield, MA	Modules/circuit boards	220	ca. 1989	M	Elamex	Cd. Juárez
General Electric		Pittsfield, MA	Wiring for the Aegis Director (U.S. military project)	60	1992	C	Electro Componentes de México	Cd. Juárez, Chihuahua
General Motors		Framingham, MA	Buick Century, Oldsmobile Ciera, Chevrolet Celebrity	1200	1989	C	General Motors de México	Ramos Arizpe
Teledyne Ryan		Dedham, MA	Microelectronics	100s	1992	C		
Black & Decker		Hampstead, MD	Power tools	100s	1987	C		Guadalajara
General Instrument	American Totalisator	Baltimore, MD	Electric components	60	1975-91	M	General Instrument de México	Guadalajara & Cd. Juárez
Cooper Industries	Arrow Hart	Lewiston, ME	Electric switches, outlets, etc.	10	1980	M	Arrow Hart & Componentes e Interruptores	Guadalajara & Cd. Juárez
Electro-Wire Products		Owosso, MI	Wire harnesses for autos	357	1990	C	Various names	Cd. Juárez (9 plants)
Ford Motor		Saline, MI	Dashboard instrumentation	400	1993-95	M	Altec Electrónica	Chihuahua

THE RUNAWAYS

From the United States . . . to Mexico

PARENT COMPANY	SUBSIDIARY	LOCATION	PRODUCT	JOBS LOST	TIME SPAN	TYPE	MEXICO COMPANY	MEXICO LOCATION
Ford Motor		Chesterfield Township, MI	Auto seat covers	800	1981-91	M	Favesa	Cd. Juárez
General Electric	GE Motor Div.	Holland, MI	Electric motors	n/a	1987-88	C		Cd. Juárez
General Mills	Lionel	Mt. Clemens, MI	Toy trains and accessories	200 ⇐	1983	C		Tijuana
Handy and Harmon	U.S. Auto Radiator	Highland Park, MI	Radiators, heater cores	180	1989	C		
Sundstrand	(now Modine Heat Transfer)	Dowagiac, MI	Heat transfer	100+	1988-89	C	Sundstrand Transferencia de Calor	Nuevo Laredo
United Technologies	Wagner Industries	Reading, MI	Auto harnesses	63	1979	C		Chihuahua (5 plants), Cd. Juárez (5 plants)
Honeywell		Plymouth & Golden Valley, MN	Building controls, thermostats	ca. 100	1990-92	M	Mexhon	Tijuana
Saft America		St. Paul, MN	Portable batteries	up to 300	1984-86		Componentes Técnicos de B.C.	Tijuana
Tonka		Mound, MN	Toys	ca. 400	1983-84	C	Juguetrenes	Cd. Juárez
Bemis	Multi-Net Div.	St. Louis, MO	Open-mesh bags	150	1987	C	Bemis Maral	San Luis Potosi
Emerson Electric	ESCO	St. Louis, MO	Wiring harnesses for printed circuit boards	35	1988-89	M	Electronica y Espacio (ESMEX)	Cd. Juárez

THE RUNAWAYS

From the United States . . . to Mexico

PARENT COMPANY	SUBSIDIARY	LOCATION	PRODUCT	JOBS LOST	TIME SPAN	TYPE	MEXICO COMPANY	MEXICO LOCATION
Falco		Kansas City & St. Louis, MO	Cast iron products	600	1987	C	Falco de México	Cd. Juárez, La Paz, Cuernavaca
General Instrument	Jerrold Communications	Kansas City, MO	Repair of cable TV convertors	200	1989-90	C	Ensambladora de Matamoros	Matamoros
Mallinckrodt Medical		New Haven, MO	Temperature monitoring systems	60	1993	C		Undecided by company
Vendo		Kansas City, MO	Soda & coffee vending machines	500+	Early 1980s	C		
Zenith Electronics		Springfield, MO	TVs & TV components	3800+	1979-92	C	Zenith de México, others	Reynosa (4 plants)
Fleck		Biloxi, MS	Power cords & wire harnesses	200	1988-92	C	Sistemas y Connecciones Integradas	Cd. Juarez
MagneTek	Universal Manufacturing	Mendenhall, MS	Light ballasts	600	1989-92	M	MagneTek Matamoros	Matamoros
Alphabet	NCA	Durham, NC	Auto wire harnesses	250	1987	C	Alfabed de México	Chihuahua
Dale Electronics		Robbinsville, NC	Computer parts	80	1990	C	Dale Electrónica	Cd. Juárez (3 plants)
Ingersoll-Rand	Schlage Lock	Rocky Mount, NC	Locks	700	1988	C	Schlage	Tecate
NACCO Industries	Proctor-Silex	Aberdeen, NC	Irons, coffeemakers, popcorn poppers	200	1991	C	Proctor-Silex de México	Cd. Juárez
NACCO Industries	Proctor-Silex	Southern Pines, NC	Irons, coffeemakers, popcorn poppers	652	1991	M	Proctor-Silex de México	Cd. Juárez

T H E   R U N A W A Y S

From the United States . . . to Mexico

PARENT COMPANY	SUBSIDIARY	LOCATION	PRODUCT	JOBS LOST	TIME SPAN	TYPE	MEXICO COMPANY	MEXICO LOCATION
R.G. Barry		Goldsboro, NC	Women's slippers	252	1991	C	R.G. Barry de México	Cd. Acuña, Nuevo Laredo, Cd. Juárez
Genicom		Hudson, NH	Computer printers	400	1989	C	Datacom de México	Reyrosa
C.R. Bard		Murray Hill, NJ	Medical supplies	230	1986	M	Productos para el Cuidado de la Salud	Nogales
Efka Plastic		Bayonne, NJ	Plastic tablecloths	225	1988	C	Plásticos Efka de México	Tiajomulco, Jalisco
Johnson & Johnson	Dental Care	East Windsor, NJ	Professional dental products	75	1988-89	C	Maquiladora Aci-Mex	Tijuana
MagneTek	Universal Manufacturing	Paterson, NJ	Light ballasts	500	1989	M	MagneTek Matamoros	Matamoros
Samsung (South Korea)	Samsung Electronics America	Saddle Brook, NJ	TV assembly	n/a		C		Tijuana
Westwood Lighting		Westwood, NJ	Desks & floor lamps	282	1987	C		Cd. Juárez
GTE	GTE Lenkurt	Albuquerque, NM	Telecommunications equipment	1800	1982-83	M		Cd. Juárez
Becton Dickinson		Hancock, NY	Intravenous tubing	n/a	1984 & 1988	M		Cd. Juárez
Combustion Engineering	Taylor Instrument	Rochester, NY	Circuit board assembly	100+	1985	M	Sistemas y Instrumentaciones	Nuevo Laredo
Cooper Industries	Cooper Power Systems	Olean, NY	Fuse links (high-voltage fuses)	15 ⇐	Mid- to late 1980s	M	Sistemas de Erergia de Matamoros	Matamoros

THE RUNAWAYS

From the United States . . . to Mexico

PARENT COMPANY	SUBSIDIARY	LOCATION	PRODUCT	JOBS LOST	TIME SPAN	TYPE	MEXICO COMPANY	MEXICO LOCATION
Ford Motor		Green Island, NY	Brass & copper heater cores	n/a	1988	M	Coclisa	Cd. Juárez
General Electric		Syracuse, NY	Cable wire & harnesses	150	1990-92	M	Electro Componentes de México	Cd. Juárez & Chihuahua
General Motors	Delco Chassis	Rochester, NY	Magnets	125	1983	M	Delredo	Nuevo Laredo
GTE-Valeron	Valenite	Syracuse, NY	Machine tools	n/a	Early 1980s	C		Mexicali
IBM		Rochester, NY	Software	6	1992	M	IBM de México	Guadalajara
Kyocera (Japan)	AVX Ceramic	Olean, NY	Ceramic capacitors	200	1985-91	M	Avio Éxito, Avio Excelente	Cd. Juárez & Chihuahua
Modern Filters		Haverstraw, NY	Fabric dust bags & filters	78	1982	C	Filtros Modernos de México	Cd. Juárez
Parker-Hannifan	Ideal Clamp Div.	Brooklyn, NY	Auto parts	300	1980-86	C	Auto Industrial de Partes	Matamoros
Quaker Oats	Fisher-Price	Holland, NY		425	1990	C		Tijuana, Acuña, Matamoros
Smith Corona		Cortland, NY	Typewriters	ca. 700	1992-93	C		Tijuana
Trico Products	Trico Components	Buffalo, NY	Windshield wipers	1200	1987-90	M		Matamoros
A.O. Smith		Upper Sandusky, OH	Electric motors	550	1981-91		10 electric motor/parts plants	Cd. Juárez & Cd. Acuña
A.O. Smith		Tipp City, OH	Electric motors	1000	1980s		10 electric motor/parts plants	Cd. Juárez & Cd. Acuña
General Electric		Cleveland, OH	Packing jobs	15	1992	M	Aparatos Electricos de Acuña	Cd. Acuña

THE RUNAWAYS

From the United States . . .   to Mexico

PARENT COMPANY	SUBSIDIARY	LOCATION	PRODUCT	JOBS LOST	TIME SPAN	TYPE	MEXICO COMPANY	MEXICO LOCATION
General Electric		Warren, OH	Handmounts for inside of light bulbs	20-50	1990-91	M	Aparatos Eléctricos de Acuña	Cd. Acuña & Monterrey
General Electric		Tiffin, OH	Hermetic motors	200	1985	C	Compañia	Cd. Juárez
General Electric	Trumbull Light	Warren, OH	Sealed beam lighting components	150	1989	C		Monterrey
General Motors		Moraine, OH	Diesel engines for pickups, vans	549	By 1995	C		Toluca
General Motors	Fisher Guide Div.	Elyria, OH	Auto seats & stamped-metal parts	600	1987	C	Rimir (Inland Fisher Guide)	Matamoros (2 plants)
General Motors	Packard Electric	Austintown, OH	Auto wire harnesses	1000	1989-93	C	Various names	19 plants
General Motors	Packard Electric Div.	Warren, OH	Auto-related electronics	4800	1974-91	M	Various names	19 plants
ITT	ITT Power Systems	Galion, OH	Telephone power systems	115	1990	C	ITT Power	Nogales
ITT	ITT Power Systems	Genoa, OH		83	1990	C	ITT Power	Nogales
Libby Owens Ford	Now owned by Pilkington Bros.	Toledo, OH	Auto windshields & flat glass	4300+	1975-95	M		
Maytag	Hoover	North Canton, OH	Low-end vacuum cleaners	100	1985	M	Juver Industrial	Cd. Juárez
Maytag	Hoover	North Canton, OH	Laundry equipment	200	1985-91	M	Hoover Mexicana	Guadalajara

THE RUNAWAYS

From the United States . . .   *to Mexico*

PARENT COMPANY	SUBSIDIARY	LOCATION	PRODUCT	JOBS LOST	TIME SPAN	TYPE	MEXICO COMPANY	MEXICO LOCATION
R.G. Barry		Columbus, OH	Slippers & women's footwear	270	1984	C	R.G. Barry de México	Cd. Acuña, Nuevo Laredo, Cd. Juárez
Siemens AG	Siemens Energy & Automation	Urbana, OH	Breakers, switchgear	10	1988		Industria de Trabajos Electricos	Cd. Juárez
Siemens AG	Siemens Energy & Automation	Bellefontaine, OH	Arc grids for circuit breakers	n/a	1987	M	Industria de Trabajos Electricos	Cd. Juárez
Square D		Oxford, OH	Circuit breakers	440	1989-90	M	Square D de México	Guadalajara
United Technologies	United Technologies Automotive	Zanesville, OH	Jig, wire, & fixture assemblies	430	1989-91		10 plants	Cd. Juárez & Chihuahua
Westinghouse		Bellefontaine, OH	Electric motors	400	1986-87	M	Manufactura de Bobinas Industriales	Cd. Juárez
Haggar Apparel		Temple, OK	Men's clothes	200	1990	C	Haggarmex, 5 others	Leon, Torreón, Guadalajara, others
Haggar Apparel		Lawton, OK	Men's clothes	290	1990	C	Haggarmex, 5 others	Leon, Torreón, Guadalajara, others
Haggar Apparel		Duncan, OK	Apparel	330	1986	C	Various names	Irapuato, Guadalajara, Torreón, Iguala, others
Zebco		Tulsa, OK	Fishing tackle, electric trolling motors	n/a ⇐	1981 & 1987	M		Cd. Juárez
BTR Dunlop PLC (UK)	Sensus Technologies	Uniontown, PA	Electronic components for gas & water meters	138	1990-91	M		Cd. Juárez

THE RUNAWAYS

From the United States . . .   *to Mexico*

PARENT COMPANY	SUBSIDIARY	LOCATION	PRODUCT	JOBS LOST	TIME SPAN	TYPE	MEXICO COMPANY	MEXICO LOCATION
Eberhard-Faber		Wilkes-Barre, PA	Pencils	100+	1986	M	Eberhard-Faber de México	Nogales
Emerson Electric	W.L. Wiegand Div.	Pittsburgh, PA	Heating elements	n/a			Wigand	Nuevo Laredo
Hanson PLC (UK)	Progress Lighting	Philadelphia, PA	Residential lighting	ca. 150	1990	C		Tijuana
Honeywell	Industrial Automation & Control Div.	Ft. Washington, PA	Electrical assembly (transmitters, valves)	75	1989	C	Honeywell de Juárez	Cd. Juárez
Philips Industries NV (Holland)	Philips Lighting	Warren, PA	Specialty lamps	200	1992	C	Componentes Eléctricos de México	Cd. Juárez
Volkswagen (Germany)		New Stanton, PA	Autos	2500	1988	C	Volkswagen de México	Puebla
Westinghouse		Beaver, PA	Safety switches	30	1987	M	Operaciones de Maquilas de Juárez	Cd. Juárez
Westinghouse		5 towns in PA	Switchgear, circuit breakers, generators	500	1980s	M	Operaciones de Maquilas de Juárez	Cd. Juárez
ACS Industries		Woonsocket, RI	Telephone cords	n/a	1987-88	M	ACS Internacional	Monterrey
Leviton Manufacturing		Warwick, RI	Wiring devices	800	1988-91		4 companies	Tijuana (2 plants), Cd. Camargo, Cd. Juárez
Kyocera (Japan)	AVX Ceramic	Conway, SC	Ceramic capacitors	100s	1984-90	M	Avio Éxito, Avio Excelente	Cd. Juárez & Chihuahua

T H E   R U N A W A Y S

From the United States . . . to Mexico

PARENT COMPANY	SUBSIDIARY	LOCATION	PRODUCT	JOBS LOST	TIME SPAN	TYPE	MEXICO COMPANY	MEXICO LOCATION
Allied-Signal	Bendix Safety Restraints	Knoxville, TN	Seat belts	1200	1986	M	American Safety Bendix, Sistemas Seguridad Bendix	Agua Prieta (2 plants), Cd. Juárez
General Electric		Memphis, TN	Auto lights	50	1990	M	Aparatos Eléctricos de Acuña	Cd. Acuña
General Electric	GE Motor Business Group	Murfreesboro, TN	Electric motors	120	1993	M		Cd. Juárez
Levi Strauss	The Jeans	Maryville, TN	Men's denim jeans	835	1988	C	Happy Jeans & Longhorn Jeans	Gómez Palacio (2 plants)
Philips Industries NV (Holland)	North American Philips	Jefferson City, TN	Electronic components for TVs & video games	1000	1982-86	M	Philips Exportadora	Cd. Juárez
Philips Industries NV (Holland)	Philips Consumer Electronics	Greeneville, TN	Small TVs (up to 20")	1500	1985-92	M	Philips Exportadora	Cd. Juárez
R.G. Barry		Chattanooga, TN	Women's slippers	150	1985	C	R.G. Barry de México	Cd. Acuña, Nuevo Laredo, Cd. Juárez
Takata		Dandridge, TN	Auto seat covers, arm- & headrests	150	1991	C		Cd. Acuña
TRW Electronics	Carr Div.	Knoxville, TN	Electronic auto parts	150	1990	C	TRW Electronics Ensambles	Reynosa
United Technologies	Carrier	Collierville, TN	Residential air conditioners	302	1990	M	Elizondo	San Nicolás, Sonora
A.C. Nielsen Co (Dun & Bradstreet)	Nielsen Clearing House	TX	Coupon processing	131	1990	C		Chihuahua, Cd. Juárez, Delicias, Nuevo Laredo, Cuauhtémoc
American Lantern		San Antonio, TX	Light fixtures (electroplated)	116	1990	C	Luces de México	Nuevo Laredo

THE RUNAWAYS

From the United States . . . to Mexico

PARENT COMPANY	SUBSIDIARY	LOCATION	PRODUCT	JOBS LOST	TIME SPAN	TYPE	MEXICO COMPANY	MEXICO LOCATION
Austin Sculpture & Decorative Art		Austin, TX	Cast sculptures	n/a	1989	C	Esculpturas Austin	Reynosa
BTK Industries/Billy The Kid	Hortex	El Paso, TX	Apparel	400	1988-89	C	Manufacturera de Ropa Laredo	Gómez Palacio (2 plants)
Cupps Henry Springer Dental Lab		Houston, TX	Dental caps, other supplies	n/a	1992	C	Reytek Internacional	Merida
Dale Electronics		El Paso, TX	Computer parts	384	1991	C	Dale Electrónica	Cd. Juárez (3 plants)
Farah Manufacturing		El Paso, TX (3 plants)	Apparel	2000+	1986-90	C		Cd. Juárez (2 plants), Chihuahua, Piedras Negras, Gómez Palacio (3 plants), Teotihuacán
General Dynamics		Fort Worth, TX	Airplane wire harnesses	300	1990-91	M	Joint venture w/ Industrias DAK	Chihuahua
Haggar Apparel		Olney, TX	Men's slacks	99	1992	C	Joint venture w/ Industrias DAK	Monterrey
Haggar Apparel		Bowie, TX	Men's slacks	259	1992	C	Joint venture w/ Industrias DAK	Monterrey
Haggar Apparel	Haggar Mens Wear/Greenville Manufacturing	Greenville, TX	Men's suits & slacks	188	1990	C	Haggarmex, 6 other plants	Leon, Torreón, Guadalajara, others
Kessler Industries		El Paso, TX	Furniture (aluminum & wood)	250	1986	M	Industrias Kessler & Maquilados Técnicos	Cd. Juárez
Levi Strauss		San Antonio, TX	Dockers trousers	1100	1990	C	Various names	Aguascalientes, Gómez Palacio (4 plants), Guadalajara

THE RUNAWAYS

From the United States . . . to Mexico

PARENT COMPANY	SUBSIDIARY	LOCATION	PRODUCT	JOBS LOST	TIME SPAN	TYPE	MEXICO COMPANY	MEXICO LOCATION
Salant	Texas Apparel	Del Rio, TX	Jeans	425	1986	C	4 maquiladoras	Cd. Acuña, Piedras Negras, Teotihuacán
Salant	Texas Apparel	Carrizo Springs, TX	Jeans	78	1990	M	4 maquiladoras	Cd. Acuña, Piedras Negras, Teotihuacán
Salant	Texas Apparel	Eagle Pass, TX	Jeans	217	1988	M	4 maquiladoras	Cd. Acuña, Piedras Negras (2 plants), Teotihuacán
Texas Instruments		Dallas, TX	Semiconductors	600+	1989-92	M	Texas Instruments de México	Aguascalientes
AT&T		Radford, VA	Communications equipment	2000	1990	C	AT&T Microelectronica	Matamoros
Cooper Industries		Earlysville, VA	Circuit breakers	100	1990-91	M	Componentes e Interruptores	Cd. Juárez
Genicom		Waynesboro, VA	Computer printers, components	90	1992	M	Datacom de México	Reynosa
Levi Strauss		Blackstone, VA	Men's jeans	265	1986	C	Happy Jeans, Longhorn Jeans	Gómez Palacio (2 plants)
Philips Industries NV (Holland)	North American Philips	Fairmont, VA	90W fluorescent lights	7	1992	M	Advance Transformers Co. de México	Cd. Juárez
Siemens AG (Germany)		Earlysville, VA	Circuit breakers	175	1992	M	Industria de Trabajo Eléctricos	Cd. Juárez
Allen-Bradley		Milwaukee, WI	Carbon composition resistors	800	1979	M	Allen-Bradley Electrónica	Cd. Juárez
Briggs & Stratton		Glendale, WI	Automotive locks	200	1987-92	C	Tecnologia Briggs y Stratton	Cd. Juárez
Brunswick	Force Outboards	Hartford, WI	Outboard motors (40+ hp)	100	1992	C	Productos Marine de México	Cd. Juárez
Chrysler	Coleman Products	Coleman, WI	Auto harnesses	450	1990	C	Coleman de Obregón	Cd. Obregón
Eaton		Milwaukee, WI	Electronic controls	58	1992	M	Condura/Apacón	Matamoros

THE RUNAWAYS

From the United States . . . *to Mexico*

PARENT COMPANY	SUBSIDIARY	LOCATION	PRODUCT	JOBS LOST	TIME SPAN	TYPE	MEXICO COMPANY	MEXICO LOCATION
Emerson Electric	U.S. Electrical Motors/Doerr Electric	Cedarburg, WI	Speed reducers for electric motors	ca. 500	1987-91	C	Motores US de México, Electrotécnia cel Norte, Compañia de Motores Domésticos	Apodaca (2 plants), Cd. Juárez
Evenflo Products	Evenflo Juvenile Furniture	Stevens Point, WI	Children's furniture	80	1991	C		Tijuana
General Motors	Delco Electronics	Oak Creek, WI	Auto-related electronics	n/a	Early 1980s	M	Delnosa, Deltronics, Delmex, etc.	Reynosa, Matamoros, Cd. Juárez
Johnson Controls		Milwaukee, WI	Heating devices	200+	1982	M	Controles Reynosa, Controles de Juarez	Reynosa, Cd. Juárez
Johnson Controls		Watertown, WI	Control devices	52	1992	M	Controles Reynosa, Controles de Juarez	Reynosa, Cd. Juárez
Kendall (Colgate-Palmolive)	Plastronics	Milwaukee, WI	Disposable medical devices, urine collection bags	285	1986	C		Tijuana
MagneTek	Louis Allis	Milwaukee, WI	Winding jobs for large electric motors	n/a	1987	M	Coil de México & IG-MEX	Matamoros & Cd. Juárez
Rockwell International	Allen-Bradley Manufacturing	M waukee, WI	Electronic components	140	1988	M	Técnica Electromecánica, Allen-Bradley Electrónica	Tecate, Cd. Juárez
Square D	Square D de México	Milwaukee, WI	Circuit breakers	up to 251	1991	C	Square D de México	Guadalajara
Sunbeam	Oster	Milwaukee, WI	Blenders, hair clippers, small appliances	ca. 200	1987	C	Sunbeam Mexicana	Cd. Acuña, Teotihuacán

THE RUNAWAYS

From the United States . . .   to Mexico

PARENT COMPANY	SUBSIDIARY	LOCATION	PRODUCT	JOBS LOST	TIME SPAN	TYPE	MEXICO COMPANY	MEXICO LOCATION
Wells Manufacturing		Fond du Lac, WI	Switches & transformers for cars	180	1989-92	M	Wells Manufacturera de México	Reynosa
West Bend		West Bend, WI	Heating controls for electrical appliances	50	1988	M		Reynosa
Philips Industries NV (Holland)	Philips Lighting	Fairmont, WV	Halogen headlights	60	1988	M	Componentes Eléctricos de México	Cd. Juárez

Methodology

In compiling Appendix A, the list of runaway jobs, we have selected a narrow definition of what constitutes "running away": a long-term net reduction in employment at a U.S. facility accompanied by an expansion of employment at a new or existing Mexican facility producing an identical or updated product or service, and controlled by the same parent company.

It should be emphasized that this definition intentionally omits three of the principal means by which U.S. jobs *indirectly* move abroad:

■ "Outsourcing." This refers to a halt in production in the United States as part of a decision to purchase certain materials or components from independent suppliers rather than producing them in-house. This problem is particularly acute in the apparel industry since a large proportion of the clothes we wear are made by subcontractors. Liz Claiborne, for example, employed only 250 people in manufacturing in 1986, relying instead on dozens of independent shops in several countries, including Mexico.[1] It would be very difficult for an outside observer to track the firm's shifting supplier base, much less to determine which shifts should be counted as runaway production.

■ Conversion from manufacturer to importer. In this extreme form of outsourcing, a company retains its distribution and marketing networks but stops manufacturing altogether. Many U.S. consumer electronics firms have taken this route. After finding their manufacturing profit margins undercut by imports, they focus on the more lucrative business of selling—often hawking their former competitors' products. Even the marketing activity can be short-lived, however; once the U.S. firms have established consumer demand for a given product, the foreign manufacturer often decides to sell its own goods under its own name, and is in a good position to undercut its U.S. partner's retail prices.

■ Declining employment due to import competition. For the apparel industry, one of the hardest hit by low-cost imports, the partial relaxation of U.S. import controls has meant that foreign garments now account for 60 percent of all apparel sold in the United States, compared to 20 percent in 1970. According to a union researcher, this surge in imports has cost U.S. workers some 425,000 jobs over last twenty years.[2]

In choosing to list only those plants where a direct production shift took place, we are also ignoring the opportunity cost to the U.S. economy of jobs created in Mexico by the expansion of activities there rather than in the United States. Thus Cummins Engine's 1991 decision to set up two new crankshaft lines in its state-of-the-art facility in San Luís Potosí rather than in Fostoria, Ohio—or at other U.S. plants that could perform the work—does not appear in our list.

Compiling the list proved to be a tremendous challenge, and it is likely that we have identified fewer than half of the U.S. work sites that lost some or all of their production jobs to Mexican plants since 1980 and that fit our conservative definition of runaways. There are a number of reasons for this:

■ Few corporations broadcast their intention to send jobs to Mexico, viewing the move as a potential public-relations liability. The response of an executive with defense contractor Teledyne Ryan to questions about his firm's two maquiladoras was typical: "The company regards (its Mexico operations) as a proprietary matter, and (company officials) have no comment."[3]

■ Runaway production rarely follows the classic pattern of a closing in the U.S. accompanied by a new facility making the same product in Mexico. Instead it often occurs through a gradual decline in orders filled by one plant and a gradual buildup of work assigned to another. Tracing such a shift may be further complicated by an upgrade of the item being produced; production of the obsolete version is allowed to taper off in one location as production of the newer model expands abroad.

■ Runaway production can happen as part of a "consolidation," "rationalization," or "restructuring" of productive activities that resembles a shell game with production being split and shuffled among numerous plants.

We began by establishing a database of foreign-owned manufacturers in Mexico whose production is geared to the U.S. market. The export orientation of the firms is crucial; we wanted to target companies that replaced U.S. workers with Mexican workers but continued to sell their products or services to the same U.S. customers. We used several directories to gather information on foreign-owned manufacturers in Mexico, but by far the most useful was *The Complete Twin Plant Guide* (El Paso, TX: SoluNet, 1991). To make the task more manageable, we excluded plants with fewer than fifty employees from our database. Despite this restriction, the list contains over 1,600 foreign-owned plants in Mexico. When available, we recorded each plant's primary products, the size of its work force, and the date it began operations.

Gathering complete and accurate data for Mexican manufacturing operations was a painstaking task, but it was even more difficult to gather systematic information about plant closings or permanent layoffs in the United States. Before 1989 employers were under no obligation to make public their layoffs or shutdowns. The Department of Labor collects data on mass layoffs, but this information is aggregated by state and industry and sheds no light on individual corporate activities. Since the Worker Adjustment and Retraining Notification (WARN) Act took effect in February 1989, each state has maintained lists of closings and large-scale layoffs. But the WARN Act is shot through with loopholes that greatly weaken its usefulness to workers and researchers. A report by the U.S. General Accounting Office found that fewer than half of all employers with more than 100 workers that closed or laid off workers during 1990 were covered by WARN, and fewer than one-third of those covered obeyed the law.[4]

From a researcher's perspective, even worse is the absence of useful information included in WARN listings and the inaccessibility of these listings to the public in several states. Only a handful of states—Wisconsin, North Carolina, and Illinois stand out—provide information about the product or industry involved in a layoff or shutdown. Nearly half fail to differentiate among shutdowns, permanent layoffs, and temporary layoffs. And ten states, including California, either refuse to release their lists in any form or make it too costly or difficult to obtain.

Lacking a systematic approach to the problem,[5] we turned to various indexes and databases covering business, industry, and general topics. We sent nearly 700 names of corporations to the DataCenter in Oakland, California, which has been cataloging plant closings across the nation since 1977. We scoured the printed indexes of major newspapers of record—including the *Wall Street Journal*, the *Washington Post*, and the *New York Times*—through the

1980s. For more recent years we used Dialog Information Services' on-line Knowledge Index, which offers complete-text access to thirty-three newspapers and abstracted references to six of the largest national papers. We also used two Predicast services—F&S Index Plus Text on CD-ROM and PTS PROMT on-line. The most productive source of information on U.S. closings and layoffs, however, was a little-known service called NewsBank, with headquarters in New Canaan, Connecticut. NewsBank's Business Journal Index offers microfiche copies of more than 200 local business-oriented publications from all fifty states, the District of Columbia, and Puerto Rico. Because they are generally based in small towns, these publications often provide details on layoffs and closings that are left out of larger papers or magazines. None of these databases features extensive coverage before the mid-1980s, unfortunately. NewsBank's Business Journal Index offers nothing at all before 1985.

We also contacted the research departments of the ten major unions we believed are most affected by the movement of manufacturing jobs to Mexico. Two of the unions—the International Brotherhood of Electrical Workers (IBEW) and the International Union of Elecronic, Electrical, Salaried, Machine and Furniture Workers (IUE)—had undertaken systematic surveys of their locals, and another—the Amalgamated Clothing and Textile Workers Union—had compiled a list of examples. The AFL-CIO had also put together a list of thirty-eight affected plants. Unfortunately, the local officials responding to the IBEW and IUE surveys—dozens of whom we interviewed—often did not know exactly where in Mexico their corporate employers had sent the work.[6]

The foregoing caveats make it clear that Appendix A represents only a small portion of the flight of U.S. jobs to Mexico. Moreover, Mexico has received only a portion of all U.S. jobs shipped abroad. Nevertheless it is an instructive list, and it illustrates the breadth of jobs and regions affected by runaway employers.

The list and the research behind it also highlight the failure of the U.S. government to collect critical information on the functioning of the national economy. Because of the crucial importance of this information to our country's economic health, we have no choice but to believe that this failure results from the desire to downplay the extent of human suffering attributable to neoliberal economic policies. We also believe that the free-market ideology that guides our economic policies contributes to this failure by refusing to acknowledge that government can and should concern itself with monitoring and ameliorating the effects of such "microeconomic" events as plant closings.

Notes

1. John H. Wilson, "And Now, the Post-industrial Corporation," *Business Week*, March 3, 1986, pp. 64-71.

2. James Parrot, "Fashioning an Industrial Strategy for Garment Workers," *Labor Research Review*, no. 19 (Fall 1992), p. 56.

3. Quoted in Elizabeth Douglass, "Defense Firms Look to Mexico," *San Diego Tribune*, May 15, 1989, p. AA-1. Some companies make a different calculation, publicizing a move to Mexico in order to gain bargaining leverage over unions or local governments, or to dramatize what they see as failings in national or state economic policies.

4. *Dislocated Workers: Worker Adjustment And Retraining Notification Act Not Meeting Its Goals, February 1993* (Washington, DC: General Accounting Office).

5. One systematic approach to tracking employment shifts within the United States would be to use Dun's Market Identifier files, which provide firm-specific information on manufacturing employment in localities across the country. This approach was used by Professor David Ranney of the University of Illinois at Chicago to document job loss at firms in the Chicago area that also operate Mexican facilities. But the expense of conducting such a survey across the country is prohibitive, and the information it generates reveals little about the reasons for job losses, giving the researcher important leads but requiring very considerable follow-up work.

6. The local officials should not be faulted for this lack of information, however. As noted earlier, corporate spokespeople frequently refuse to reveal where production is moving, and often flat out lie about its destination or the reasons for a cutback. One industrious unionist at AT&T's Radford, Virginia, plant was forced to play detective with the company's shipping invoices to confirm his suspicion that an AT&T facility in Mexico was producing parts that had formerly been made in Radford. See Michael Martz, "Union's Charge About Mexico Has Deep Effect," *Richmond Times-Dispatch*, Aug. 16, 1992, p. E-1.

Resources

Books and Reports

Adams, Frank T., and Gary B. Hansen. *Putting Democracy to Work: A Practical Guide for Starting and Managing Worker-Owned Businesses.* San Francisco: Berrett-Koehler Publishers, 1992.

Alliance for Responsible Trade. *Development and Trade Strategies for North America.* Washington, DC: Alliance for Responsible Trade, 1991. 100 Maryland Ave. NE, Box 74, Washington, DC 20002. Tel: (202) 544-7198.

American Federation of Grain Millers, AFL-CIO CLC. *The Grain Millers' Role in Creating Labor/Management Partnerships for New Work Systems.* Minneapolis: American Federation of Grain Millers, AFL-CIO CLC. 4949 Olson Memorial Highway, Minneapolis, MN 55422. Tel: (612) 545-0211.

American Labor Education Center. *$4 A Day/No Way!* Washington, DC: American Labor Education Center, 1991.

Anderson, Mark. *Labor Rights and Standards and the NAFTA.* Washington, DC: AFL-CIO, Dec. 3, 1992. 815 16th St. NW, Washington, DC 20006. Tel: (202) 637-5187.

———. *Minimum Wages and the NAFTA.* Washington, DC: AFL-CIO. 815 16th St. NW, Washington, DC 20006. Tel: (202) 637-5187.

Barlett, Donald, and James Steele. *America: What Went Wrong?* Kansas City: Andrews and McMeel, 1992.

Bello, Walden. *Brave New Third World.* San Francisco: Food First, 1988.

Bluestone, Barry, and Bennett Harrison. *Capital and Communities: The Causes and Consequences of Private Disinvestment.* Washington, DC: The Progressive Alliance, 1980.

———. *The Deindustrialization of America: Plant Closings, Community Abandonment, and the Dismantling of Basic Industry.* New York: Basic Books, 1982.

Bowles, Samuel, David M. Gordon, and Thomas E. Weisskopf. *After the Waste Land: A Democratic Economics for the Year 2000.* Armonk, NY: M.E. Sharpe Inc., 1990.

Brecher, Jeremy, John Brown Childs, and Jill Cutler, eds. *Global Visions: Beyond the New World Order.* Boston: South End Press, 1993.

——— and Tim Costello. *Building Bridges: The Emerging Grassroots Coalition of Labor and Community.* New York: Monthly Review Press, 1990.

———. *Global Village vs. Global Pillage: A One-World Strategy for Labor.* Washington, DC: International Labor Rights Education and Research Fund. 100 Maryland Ave. NE, Box 74, Washington, DC 20002. Tel: (202) 544-7198.

Cantor, Daniel, and Juliet Schor. *Tunnel Vision: Labor, the World Economy, and Central America.* Boston: South End Press, 1987.

Cavanagh, John, John Gershman, Karen Baker, and Gretchen Helmke, eds. *Trading Freedom: How Free Trade Affects our Lives, Work, and Environment.* San Francisco: Institute for Food and Development Policy. 145 9th St., San Francisco, CA 94103.

————, Lance Compa, Allan Ebert, Bill Goold, Kathy Selvaggio, and Tim Shorrock. *Trade's Hidden Costs: Worker Rights in a Changing World Economy.* Washington, DC: International Labor Rights Education and Research Fund, 1988. 100 Maryland Ave. NE, Box 74, Washington, DC 20002.

Center for Popular Economics. *Creating a New World Economy: Forces for Change and Plans for Action.* Amherst: Center for Popular Economics, forthcoming. Box 785, Amherst, MA, 01004. Tel: (413) 545-0743.

Commission on the Skills of the American Workforce. *America's Choice: High Skills or Low Wages!* Rochester, NY: National Center on Education and the Economy, 1990.

Dawkins, Kristin. *Trade Policy and International Democracy: Seeking a Citizens' Role in Dispute Resolution.* Available from Institute for Agriculture and Trade Policy, 1212 5th St. SE #303, Minneapolis, MN 55414. Tel: (612) 379-5980.

Doherty, Barbara. *The Struggle to Save Morse Cutting Tool: A Successful Community Campaign.* North Dartmouth: Labor Education Center, 1986. Southeastern Massachusetts University, North Dartmouth, MA 12747.

Dorman, Peter. *Worker Rights and U.S. Trade Policy.* Washington, DC: U.S. Department of Labor, 1989.

Economic Strategy Institute. *Free Trade with Mexico: The Potential Economic Impact.* Washington, DC: Economic Strategy Institute, May 1991.

Faux, Jeff, and William Spriggs. *U.S. Jobs and the Mexico Trade Proposal.* Washington, DC: Economic Policy Institute, May 1991.

Fenton, Thomas, and Mary Heffron, eds. *Transnational Corporations and Labor: A Directory of Resources.* Maryknoll, NY: Orbis Books, 1989.

General Accounting Office. *Plant Closings: Limited Advance Notice and Assistance Provided Dislocated Workers.* Washington, DC: General Accounting Office, 1987.

Grunwald, Joseph, and Kenneth Flamm, eds. *The Global Factory: Foreign Assembly in International Trade.* Washington, DC: Brookings, 1985.

Haas, Gilda. *Plant Closures: Myths, Realities, Responses.* Boston: South End Press, 1985.

Harrison, Bennett, and Barry Bluestone. *The Great U-Turn: Corporate Restructuring and the Polarizing of America.* New York: Basic Books, 1988.

Harvey, Pharis. *Protecting Labor Rights in Connection with North American Trade.* Statement before the U.S. House of Representatives Committee on Ways and Means, March 11, 1993. International Labor Rights Education and Research Fund. 100 Maryland Ave. NE, Box 74, Washington, DC 20002. Tel: (202) 544-7198.

Hecker, Steven, and Margaret Hallock, eds. *Labor in a Global Economy.* Eugene: University of Oregon Books, 1991.

Hernández, Ricardo, and Edith Sánchez. *Cross-Border Links: A Directory of Organizations in Canada, Mexico, and the United States.* Albuquerque, NM: Inter-Hemispheric Education Resource Center, 1992.

Herzenberg, Stephen, and Jorge F. Perez-Lopez, eds. *Labor Standards and Development in the Global Economy.* Washington, DC: U.S. Department of Labor, 1990.

ICFTU/ORIT International Conference. *Economic Integration, Development, and Democracy.* Washington, DC: AFL-CIO. 815 16th St. NW, Washington, DC 20006. Tel: (202) 637-5187.

Illinois Advisory Committee to the United States Commission on Civil Rights. *Shutdown: Economic Dislocation and Equal Opportunity.* Chicago, June 1981.

Kamel, Rachael. *The Global Factory: Analysis and Action for a New Economic Era.* Philadelphia: American Friends Service Committee, 1990.

Kerson, Roger, and Greg LeRoy. *State and Local Initiatives on Development Subsidies and Plant Closings.* Chicago: Federation for Industrial Retention and Renewal, 1989. 3411 W. Diversey Ave. #10, Chicago, IL 60647. Tel: (312) 278-5418.

Kochan, Leslie. *Maquiladoras and Toxics: The Hidden Costs of Production South of the Border.* Washington, DC: AFL-CIO, 1989. 815 16th St. NW, Washington, DC 20006. Tel: (202) 637-5187.

Labor Advisory Committee for Trade Negotiations and Trade Policy. *Labor Advisory Committee on The North American Free Trade Agreement.* Washington, DC, Sept. 16, 1992. Available from AFL-CIO, 815 16th St. NW, Washington, DC 20006. Tel: (202) 637-5178.

LaBotz, Dan. "A Troublemaker's Handbook: How to Fight Back Where You Work—And Win!" Detroit: Labor Notes, Jan. 1991.

———. *The Mask of Democracy: Labor Suppression in Mexico Today.* Boston: South End Press, 1992.

LeRoy, Greg, Dan Swinney, and Elaine Charpentier. *Early Warning Manual Against Plant Closings.* Chicago: Midwest Center for Labor Research, 1988. 3411 W. Diversey Ave. #10, Chicago, IL 60647. Tel: (312) 278-5418.

Levinson, Jerome I. *Unrequited Toil: Denial of Labor Rights in Mexico and Implications for NAFTA.* New York: World Policy Institute, April 1993.

Marks, Siegfried. *Miami Report III: Recommendations for a North American Free Trade Agreement and for Future Hemispheric Trade.* Miami: University of Miami, 1992. The North-South Center, Box 248205, Coral Gables, FL 33124-3027. Tel: (305) 284-8914.

Marshall, Ray. *Unheard Voices: Labor and Economic Policy in a Competitive World.* New York: Basic Books, 1987.

Mead, Walter Russell. *The Low-Wage Challenge to Global Growth.* Washington, DC: Economic Policy Institute, 1990.

Melman, Seymour. *What Else is There to Do?: Neglected Prospects for Major New Employment in U.S. Manufacturing.* Report to the National Commission for Economic Conversion and Disarmament, forthcoming, 1993. 1801 18th St. NW, Washington, DC 20009. Tel: (202) 462-0091.

Mishel, Lawrence, and David M. Frankel. *The State of Working America: 1990-91.* Armonk, NY: M.E. Sharpe Inc., 1991.

——— and R.A. Teixeira. *The Myth of the Coming Labor Shortage: Jobs, Skills and Incomes of America's Workforce 2000.* Washington, DC: Economic Policy Institute, 1990.

Mobilization on Development, Trade, Labor and the Environment. *Development and Trade Strategies for North America.* Washington, DC: Mobilization on Development, Trade, Labor and the Environment, Jan. 1992. Available from Alliance for Responsible Trade, 100 Maryland Ave. NE, Box 74, Washington, DC 20002. Tel: (202) 544-7198.

Moody, Kim, and Mary McGinn. "Unions and Free Trade: Solidarity vs. Competition." Detroit: Labor Notes, Jan. 1991.

Morris, David. *Trading Our Future: Talking Back to GATT.* St. Paul, MN: Institute for Local Self-Reliance. 220 West King St., St. Paul, MN 55107.

———. *Free Trade: the Great Destroyer.* St. Paul, MN: Institute for Local Self-Reliance. 220 West King St., St. Paul, MN 55107.

National Labor Committee Education Fund. *Paying to Lose Our Jobs: In Support of Worker and Human Rights in Central America.* Sept. 1992. ACTWU, 15 Union Square West, New York, NY 10003-3377. Tel: (212) 242-0700.

Parker, Mike, and Jane Slaughter. *Choosing Sides, Unions and the Team Concept.* Boston: South End Press, 1988.

Perich-Anderson, J., K. Boyle, L. Palki-McDowell, D. Hutchinson, and K. Wilson. *Joint Labor Management Process: A Workbook for Union Representatives.* Washington, DC: Communications Workers of America. 501 3rd St., Washington, DC 20001-2797. Tel: (202) 434-1185.

Prosten, Richard. "The Longest Season: Union Organizing in the Last Decade, a/k/a How Come One Team Has to Play With Their Shoelaces Tied Together?" Proceedings, 31st Annual Meeting, Industrial Relations Research Association, Madison, WI: IRRA, 1979.

Rachleff, Peter. *Hard-Pressed in the Heartland: The Hormel Strike and the Future of the Movement.* Boston: South End Press, 1993.

Rothstein, Richard. *Setting the Standard: International Labor Rights and U.S. Trade Policy.* Washington, DC: Economic Policy Institute, March 12, 1993. 1730 Rhode Island Ave. NW #200, Washington, DC 20036. Tel: (202) 775-8810.

Sarmiento, Anthony, and Ann Kay. *Worker-Centered Learning: A Union Guide to Workplace Literacy.* Washington, DC: AFL-CIO, Dec. 3, 1992. 815 16th St. NW, Washington, DC 20006. Tel: (202) 638-3912.

Sklair, Leslie. *Assembling for Development: The Maquila Industry in Mexico and the United States.* Winchester, MA: Unwin Hyman, 1989.

Stern, Robert, K. Haydn Wood, and Tove Hammer. *Employee Ownership in Plant Shutdowns: Prospects for Employment Stability.* Kalamazoo, MI: The W.E. Upjohn Institute for Employment Research, 1979.

Swinney, Dan, Miguel Vazquez, and Howard Engelskirschen. *Towards a New Vision of Community Economic Development.* Distributed by Midwest Center for Labor Research, 3411 W. Diversey Ave. #10, Chicago, IL 60647. Tel: (312) 278-5418.

Tennessee Industrial Renewal Network. *Taking Charge: A Hands on Guide to Dealing with the Threat of Plant Closings and Supporting Laid-off Workers.* Knoxville: Tennessee Industrial Renewal Network. 1515 E. Magnolia Ave. #408, Knoxville, TN 37917. Tel: (615) 637-1576.

Transnational Information Exchange. *Meeting the Corporate Challenge: A Handbook on Corporate Campaigns.* Amsterdam: Transnational Information Exchange, 1985. Paulus Potterstraat 20, 1071 DA Amsterdam, The Netherlands. Tel: 020-766-724.

United Auto Workers. *Your Right to be WARNed.* Detroit: United Auto Workers. 8000 E. Jefferson Ave., Detroit, MI 48214. Tel: (313) 926-5291

U.S. Citizen's Analysis of the North American Free Trade Agreement. Washington, DC: Development GAP, Dec. 1992. 1400 I St. NW #520, Washington, DC 20005. Tel: (202) 898-1566.

U.S. Congress, Office of Technology Assessment. *Worker Training: Competing in the New International Economy.* Washington, DC: Government Printing Office, 1990.

———. *Plant Closing: Advance Notice and Rapid Response.* Washington, DC: Government Printing Office, 1986.

———. *Technology and Structural Unemployment: Reemploying Displaced Adults.* Washington, DC: Government Printing Office, 1986.

———. *U.S.-Mexico Trade: Pulling Together or Pulling Apart?* Washington, DC: Government Printing Office, Oct. 1992.

U.S. International Trade Commission. *The Use and Economic Impact of TSUS Items 806.30 and 807.00.* Washington, DC: U.S. International Trade Commission, 1988.

Wachtel, Howard. *The Money Mandarins: The Making of a Supranational Economic Order.* New York: Pantheon Books, 1986.

Wintner, Linda. "Employee Buyouts: An Alternative to Plant Closings." *Research Bulletin* (New York), no. 140 (1983).

Witt, Matt. "An Injury to One is Un Agravio a Todos: The Need for a Mexico-U.S. Health and Safety Movement." *New Solutions: A Journal of Environmental and Occupational Health Policy* (Winter 1991). Available from Institute for Agriculture and Trade Policy, 1313 5th St. SE #303, Minneapolis, MN 55414. Tel: (612) 379-5980.

Periodicals

Beyond Borders: A Forum for Labor in Action around the Globe. Beyond Borders, 4677 30th St. #214, San Diego, CA 92116. Tel: (619) 280-2976.

Correspondencia (quarterly). Mujer a Mujer, Box 12322, San Antonio, TX 78212.

El Cotidiano (6x yearly). Universidad Autónoma Metropolitana, Unidad Azcapotzalco. División de Ciencias Sociales y Humanidades, Apartado Postal 32-031, México 06031, D.F. Tel: (5) 3-82-50-00, ext. 151.

CrossRoads (monthly). Especially "The Global Economy: Unions, Workers, Borders," no 12, July-Aug. 1991. Box 2809, Oakland, CA 94609.

Dollars and Sense (monthly). Economic Affairs Bureau, 1 Summer St., Somerville, MA 02143. Tel: (617) 628-8411.

Economic Notes: News and Analysis for Trade Unionists (monthly). Labor Research Association, 145 W. 28th St., 6th Floor, New York, NY 10001-6191. Tel: (212) 714-1677 or (800) 875-8775.

FIRR Notes (published 9 times yearly). Provides background and organizing information on plant closures, fight-back campaigns, dislocated worker assistance programs, economic development, and similar issues. The Aug. 1992 issue is an organizing guide to cross-border worker exchanges. Federation for Industrial Retention and Renewal, 3411 W. Diversey Ave. #10, Chicago, IL 60647. Tel: (312) 252-7676.

Labor Notes (monthly). 7435 Michigan Ave., Detroit, MI 48210. Tel: (313) 842-6262.

Labor Research Review (biannual). Provides a forum for community and labor activists to communicate their ideas and experience to a wider audience. Midwest Center for Labor Research, 3411 W. Diversey Ave. #10, Chicago, IL 60647. Tel: 312-278-5418. Especially *Solidarity Across Borders: U.S. Labor in a Global Economy* (no. 13, Spring 1989); *Participating in Management: Union Organizing on a New Terrain* (no. 14, Summer 1989); and *Saving Manufacturing: Charting a New Course For Our Unions and Communities* (no. 19, Fall 1992).

NAFTAThoughts (6x yearly). Development GAP, 1400 I St. NW #520, Washington, DC 20005. Tel: (202) 898-1612.

The Other Side of Mexico (6x yearly). Equipo Pueblo, Francisco Field Jurado 51, Colonia Independencia, México, D.F. 03630. Tel: (5) 5-39-00-15.

Report on the Americas (5x yearly). North American Congress on Latin America (NACLA), 475 Riverside Dr. #454, New York, NY 10115. Tel: (212) 870-3146.

Southern Exposure. Especially "Everybody's Business: A People's Guide to Economic Development." *Southern Exposure* 14, nos. 5-6. 604 W. Chapel St., Durham, NC 27701. Tel: (919) 688-8167.

Trade Union Advisor (biweekly). Labor Research Association, 145 W. 28th St., 6th Floor, New York, NY 10001-6191. Tel: (212) 714-1677.

Tradeswomen. PO Box 40664, San Francisco, CA 94140

Worker Rights News (quarterly). International Labor Rights Education and Research Fund, 100 Maryland Ave. NE, Box 74, Washington, DC 20002. Tel: (202) 544-7198.

Z Magazine (11x yearly). 116 St. Botolph St., Boston, MA 02115-9979.

Audio-Visual

The Business of America. This film challenges the assumption that maximization of corporate profit will lead to economic well-being among U.S. workers. It considers alternative strategies for accountable economic decision making, such as worker ownership, targeted pension fund investment, and regional economic planning. 45 minutes, 1984. California Newsreel, 149 9th St. #420, San Francisco, CA 94103. Tel: (415) 621-6522.

Caterpillar: A Story of a Plant Closure. Documentary on workers in Toronto, Ontario. 30 minutes. Canadian Broadcasting Corporation, Film Library, Box 500 Station A, Toronto, ON M5W 1E6 Canada. Tel: (416) 205-6693.

Dirty Business: Food Exports to the United States. Documentary on Green Giant's relocation of vegetable-processing operations from California to Mexico. 15 minutes, 1990. Migrant Media Productions, Box 2048, Freedom, CA 95019.

$4 a Day?/ No Way! 20 minutes, 1991. American Labor Education Center, 2000 P St. NW #300, Washington, DC 20036. Tel: (202) 828-5170.

Jobs with Justice: The Economic and Political World We Organize In. Slide presentation for unions and labor-community coalitions. 501 3rd St. NW, Washington, DC 20001.

Labor Beat. Television show and instructional resource for making your own video or cable-access show. Project of the Committee for Labor Access on TV. 37 S. Ashland St., Chicago, IL 60607. Tel: (312) 226-3330.

Roger and Me. Humorous perspective on the real-world effects of plant closings on people and communities. 106 minutes. Available at most video-rental stores.

Stepan Chemical: The Poisoning of a Mexican Community. Outlines the efforts of colonia residents in Matamoros, Mexico, and the Coalition for Justice in the Maquiladoras to pressure Stepan Chemical Company to clean up the site of its chemical plant. Coalition for Justice in the Maquiladoras, 3120 W. Ashby, San Antonio, TX 78228. Tel: (210) 732-8957.

Trading our Future? 20 minutes, 1990. Fair Trade Campaign, Midwest Regional Office, 220 S. State St. #714, Chicago, IL 60604. Tel: (312) 341-4713.

We Do the Work. 2531 9th St., Berkeley, CA 94710. Tel: (510) 549-0775. Nationwide monthly TV show on working people's issues appearing on public TV channels.

Organizations Working to Establish Fair Trade

The following groups are leaders in the effort to ensure that international economic agreements do not promote competitive strategies based on low standards or repressed wages. The listing includes groups that focus on strengthening cross-border relations among labor and other grassroots activists. For reasons of length, we have excluded the many unions contributing to this effort. For a comprehensive directory of organzations in Canada, Mexico, and the United States that are engaged in cross-border activities, see the Resource Center's *Cross-Border Links.*

Action Canada Network
904-251 Laurier Ave. West
Ottawa, ON K1P 5J6 Canada
Tel: (613) 233-1764
Fax: (613 233-1458

Alliance for Responsible Trade (ART, formerly MODTLE)
100 Maryland Ave. NE, Box 74
Washington, DC 20002
Tel: (202) 544-7198
Fax: (202) 544-7213 (202) 543-5999
Email (Peacenet): laborrights

American Friends Service Committee
Maquiladora Project
Women and Global Corporations Project
U.S.-Mexico Border Program
1501 Cherry St.
Philadelphia, PA 19102
Tel: (215) 241-7132
Fax: (215) 241-7275

American Labor Education Center
2000 P St. NW #300
Washington, DC 20036
Tel: (202) 828-5170
Fax: (202) 828-5173
Email (PeaceNet): alec

Citizens Trade Campaign
600 Maryland Ave. SW
Washington, DC 20024
Tel: (202) 554-1102
Fax: (202) 554-1654

Coalition for Justice in the Maquiladoras
3120 W. Ashby
San Antonio, TX 78228
Tel: (512) 732-8957
Fax: (512) 732-8324

Development GAP (Development Group for Alternative Policy)
1400 I St. NW #520
Washington, DC 20005
Tel: (202) 898-1566

Economic Policy Institute
1730 Rhode Island Ave. NW #812
Washington, DC 20036
Tel: (202) 775-8810

Equipo Pueblo
A.P. 27-467
Mexico, D.F. 06760
Tel: (5) 5-39-00-15
Fax: (5) 6-72-74-53
Email (PeaceNet): igc:pueblo

Fair Trade Campaign
Midwest Regional Office
220 S. State St. #714
Chicago, IL 60604
Tel: (312) 341-4713
Fax: (312) 341-4716
Email: iatp

Western Regional Office
425 Mississippi St.
San Francisco, CA 94107
Tel: (415) 826-6314
Fax: (415) 826-5303

Eastern Regional Office
410 W. 25th St.
New York, NY 10001
Tel: (212) 627-2314
Fax: (212) 366-4312

Southern Regional Office
233 Mitchell St. SW #525
Atlanta, Georgia 30303
Tel: (404) 524-4116
Fax: (404) 524-4116

Farm Labor Organizing Committee (FLOC)
507 S. St. Clair St.
Toledo, OH 43602
Tel: (419) 243-3456
Fax: (419) 243-5655

Frente Auténtico del Trabajo (FAT) Authentic Labor Front
No. 20 Calle Godard
Colonia Guadalupe Victoria]
México, D.F. 07790
Tel: (5) 5-56-93-14
Fax: (5) 5-56-93-16
Email (PeaceNet): igc:rmalc

Interfaith Center for Corporate Responsibility
475 Riverside Dr. #566
New York, NY 10115-0050
Tel: (212) 870-2984
Fax: (212) 870-2023

International Labor Rights Education and Research Fund (ILRERF)
100 Maryland Ave. NE, Box 74
Washington, DC 20002
Tel: (202) 544-7198
Fax: (202) 543-5999
Email (PeaceNet): laborrights

Labor Center/Evergreen State College Labor Education Center
Evergreen State College
Olympia, WA 98505
Tel: (206) 866-6000
Fax: (206) 866-6798

Labor Education and Research Center
University of Oregon
1675 Agate St.
Eugene, OR 97403-1289
Tel: (503) 346-5054
Fax: (503) 346-2790

Mexico-U.S. Diálogos Program
103 Washington St. #8
New York, NY 10006
Tel: (212) 233-0155
Fax: (212) 233-0238

Mobilization on Development, Trade, Labor, and the Environment
(See Alliance for Responsible Trade)

Mujer a Mujer
Mexican Office
A.P. 24-553
Colonia Roma
Mexico, D.F. 03201
Tel: (011) 525-207-0834
Email (PeaceNet): igc:mam

U.S. Office
P.O. Box 12322
San Antonio, TX 78212, USA

Canadian Office
606 Shaw St.
Toronto, ON M6G 3L6 Canada
Tel: (416) 532-8584

National Labor Committee Education Fund
c/o ACTWU
15 Union Square West
New York, NY 10003
Tel: (212) 242-0700

National Lawyer's Guild Labor and Employment Committee
811 1st Ave. #650
Seattle, WA 98104
Tel: (206) 624-7364
Fax: (206) 624-8226

North American Worker-to-Worker Network (NAWWN)
PO Box 1943
Rocky Mount, NC 27802
Tel: (919) 985-1957
Fax: (919) 985-2052

Red Mexicana de Acción Frente al Libre Comercio (RMALC)/Mexican Action Network on Free Trade
No. 20 Calle Godard
Colonia Guadalupe Victoria
México, D.F. 07790
Tel: (5) 5-56-93-14
Fax: (5) 5-56-93-16
Email (PeaceNet): igc:rmalc

Transnational Information Exchange (TIE)
7435 Michigan Ave.
Detroit, MI 48210
Tel: (313) 842-6262
Fax: (313) 842-0227
Email (PeaceNet): igc:labornotes

U.S./Guatemala Labor Education Project
c/o ACTWU-Chicago Joint Board
333 S. Ashland Ave.
Chicago, IL 60607
Tel: (312) 262-6502
Fax: (312) 262-6602
Email (PeaceNet): igc:usglep

Organizations Working to Halt Runaway Plants

The following groups have valuable experience in combatting plant closures and relocations, primarily on the local or regional levels.

Black Workers for Justice
PO Box 1863
Rocky Mount, NC 27802
Tel: (919) 977-8162

Center for Community Change
1000 Wisconsin Ave. NW
Washington, DC 20007
Tel: (202) 342-0519
Fax: (202) 342-1132

Center for Economic Conversion
222 View St. #C
Mountain View, CA 94041
(415) 968-8798

Center for Popular Economics
PO Box 785
Amherst, MA 01004
Tel: (413) 545-0743

DataCenter
464 19th St.
Oakland, CA 94612
Tel: (415) 835-4692

Federation for Industrial Retention and Renewal (FIRR)
3411 W. Diversey Ave #10
Chicago, IL 60647
Tel: (312) 252-7676
Tel: (312) 252-8797 (Trade Issues)
Fax: (312) 278-5918
Email (PeaceNet): igc:firr

Highlander Research and Education Center
1959 Highlander Way
New Market, TN 37802
Tel: (615) 933-3443
Fax: (615) 933-3424
Email (EcoNet): jmcalevey

Jane and Maurice Sugar Law Center
National Lawyers Guild Project
2915 Cadillac Tower
Detroit, MI 48226
Tel: (313) 962-6540

La Mujer Obrera
114 Poplar St.
El Paso, TX 79901
Tel: (915) 533-9710

Labor-Community Strategy Center
14540 Haynes St.
Van Nuys, CA 91411
Tel: (818) 781-4800

Labor Education and Research Project
(Labor Notes)
7435 Michigan Ave.
Detroit, MI 48210
Tel: (313) 842-6262
Fax: (313) 842-0227
Email (PeaceNet): igc:labornotes

Labor Research Association
145 W. 28th St.
New York, NY 10001
Tel: (212) 714-1677
Fax: (212) 714 1674

Midwest Center for Labor Research
3411 W. Diversey Ave. #10
Chicago, IL 60647
Tel: (312) 278-5418
Fax: (312) 278-5918

Plant Closures Project
3313 Grand Ave. #102
Oakland, CA 97610
Tel: (510) 465-7531
Fax: (510) 465-7532

Southerners for Economic Justice
Box 240
Durham, NC 27702
Tel: (919) 683-1361

Tennessee Industrial Renewal Network
(TIRN)
1515 E. Magnolia Ave. #408
Knoxville, TN 37917
Tel: (615) 637-1576

Wisconsin Regional Training
Partnership
Milwaukee HIRE Center
838 W. National Ave.
Milwaukee, WI 53204
Tel: (414) 649-4820
Fax: (414) 649-4830

Consultants on Worker Ownership

This directory contains groups that either specialize in worker ownership or use worker ownership as one alternative to plant closings.

AFL-CIO ESOP Group (currently
organizing)
c/o John Zalusky
AFL-CIO Research Department
815 16th St. NW
Washington, DC 20006
Tel: (202) 637-5000

American Capital Strategies
3 Bethesda Metro Center
Bethesda, MD 20814
Tel: (301) 951-6122
Fax: (301) 654-6714
Investment firm.

Brody & Weiser
21 Woodland St.
New Haven, CT 06511
Tel: (203) 777-5375

California Department of Commerce
801 K St. #1700
Sacramento, CA 95814
Tel: (916) 322-1398

Center for Community Self-Help
Box 3259
Durham, NC 27705
Tel: (919) 683-3019

Center for Economic Organizing
1522 K St. NW #406
Washington, DC 20005
Tel: (202) 775-9072
Fax: (202) 775-9074

**(CESCO) Community Economic
Stabilization Corporation**
522 5th SW #110
Portland, OR 97204
Tel: (503) 228-2865

The ESOP Association
1726 M St. NW #501
Washington, DC 20036
Tel: (202) 293-2971

Federation of Southern Cooperatives
Box 95
Epes, AL 35460
Tel: (205) 652-9676

Foundation for Enterprise Development
Box 2149
La Jolla, CA 92038
Tel: (619) 459-4662
Or:
8300 Greensboro Dr. #1201
McLean, VA 22102
Tel: (703) 749-9080

**Hawaii Department of Economic
Development**
Box 2359
Honolulu, HI 96804
Tel: (808) 586-2593

**Illinois Development Finance Authority
(IDFA)**
2 N. La Salle
Chicago, IL 60602
Tel: (312) 793-5586

**ICA Group (Industrial Cooperative
Association)**
20 Park Plaza #1127
Boston, MA 02116
Tel: (617) 338-0010

Labor-Community Strategy Center
14540 Haynes St.
Van Nuys, CA 91411
Tel: (818) 781-4800

**Law Firm of Ball, Hayden, Kiernan,
Livingston & Smith**
108 Washington St.
Newark, NJ 07102
(201) 622-3278

Locker Associates
195 Broadway, 7th Floor
New York, NY 10038
Tel: (212) 962-2983

**Massachusetts Industrial Services
Program**
Office of Employee Involvement and
Ownership
100 Cambridge St. #1302
Boston, MA 02202
Tel: (617) 727-8158

Midwest Employee Ownership Center
2550 West Grand Blvd.
Detroit, MI 48208
Tel: (313) 894-1066

Montana Department of Commerce
1424 9th Ave.
Helena, MT 59620
Tel: (406) 444-3494

**Office of Financial and Management
Assistance**
New Jersey Department of Commerce
20 W. State St. CN 823
Trenton, NJ 08625
Tel: (609) 984-3409

**New York Center for Employee
Ownership and Participation**
Industrial Cooperation Council
1515 Broadway, 52nd Floor
New York, NY 10036
Tel: (212) 930-0108

**National Center for Employee
Ownership**
2201 Broadway #807
Oakland, CA 94612
Tel: (510) 272-9461
Fax: (510) 272-9510

**New York Center for Employee
Ownership**
151 Broadway St.
New York, NY 10036
Tel: (212) 827-6192

Northeast Ohio Employee Ownership Center
Kent State University
Kent, OH 44242
Tel: (216) 672-3028

Pennsylvania Employee Ownership Assistance Program
Pennsylvania Department of Commerce
494 Forum Building
Harrisburg, PA 17120
Tel: (717) 787-7120

PRAXIS
133 S. 18th St., 3rd Floor
Philadelphia, PA 19103
Tel: (215) 561-5192

Program for Employment and Workplace Systems
School of Industrial and Labor Relations
Box 1000, Ives Hall
Cornell University
Ithaca, NY 14853
Tel: (202) 256-4530

Puget Sound Cooperative Federation
4201 Roosevelt St. NE
Seattle, WA 98105
Tel: (206) 632-4559

Seattle Worker Center
2411 Western Ave.
Seattle, WA 98121
Tel:(206) 634-2222

Steel Valley Authority
120 E. 9th Ave.
Homestead, PA 15120
Tel: (412) 462-8408

Utah State University Business and Economic Development Services
UMC 35, Box 95923
Logan, UT 84322
Tel: (801) 750-2283

Washington Employee Ownership Program
Department of Community and Economic Development
Ninth and Columbia Building
Mail Stop GH-51
Olympia, WA 98504-4151
Tel: (206) 586-8984

Wisconsin Cooperative Development Council
30 W. Mifflin St. #401
Madison, WI 53703
Tel: (608) 258-4396

Wisconsin Department of Development
Box 7970
Madison, WI 53703
Tel: (608) 258-4396

Resource Center Press

Resource Center Press is the imprint of the Inter-Hemispheric Education Resource Center, a private, nonprofit, research and policy institute located in Albuquerque, New Mexico. Founded in 1979, the Resource Center produces books, policy reports, audiovisuals, and other educational materials about U.S. foreign policy, as well as sponsoring popular education projects. For more information and a catalog of publications, please write to the Resource Center, Box 4506, Albuquerque, New Mexico 87196.

Board of Directors

Mexico: A Country Guide

THE ESSENTIAL SOURCE ON MEXICAN SOCIETY, ECONOMY, AND POLITICS

One of our best sellers, *Mexico: A Country Guide* is the only comprehensive book about Mexican society, politics, and economy in the 1990s—an invaluable resource for students, academics, and anyone interested in the interrelationship between our two countries. Includes photos, tables, charts, references, and index.

"**Easily the best source book on contemporary Mexican society.**" – Choice: Current Reviews for College Libraries

"**Extremely useful. . . . It goes beyond press reports and hyperbole, providing a balanced overall and insightful analysis of the most recent changes in Mexico. Indispensable for anybody who wants to understand, do business with, or simply get to know Mexico.**" – Jorge Castañeda, Political Science, National Autonomous University of Mexico

Edited by Tom Barry
1992. Paperback, 401 pages. ISBN 0-911213-35-X. $14.95
Spanish edition: ISBN 968-6217-008, $19.95

Cross-Border Links

A DIRECTORY OF ORGANIZATIONS IN CANADA, MEXICO, AND THE UNITED STATES

This invaluable and timely directory provides an annotated listing of all educational, social justice, labor, scholarly, and business groups with a special interest in relations between Mexico, Canada, and the United States. *Cross-Border Links* lists each organization's name, description of activity, key contact, address, phone, and publications.

"**As Mexico, the United States, and Canada enter a new era of collaboration and partnership, this directory represents the definitive listing of many groups, organizations, and agencies working on cross-border issues.**" – San Diego Mayor's Office of Binational Affairs

Second printing, July 1993. Paperback, 257 pages
ISBN 0-911213-38-4. $14.95

TO ORDER: *Shipping and handling charges within the U.S. are $3 for the first book, 50¢ for each additional. For shipment by ground to international locations, include $4 for the first book, $1.50 for each additional. Send check or money order to: Resource Center, Box 4506, Albuquerque, NM 87196. Order by phone using Visa/Mastercard: (505) 842-8288. Prices subject to change.*

Workers of the World Undermined

AMERICAN LABOR'S ROLE IN U.S. FOREIGN POLICY

This publication blows the lid off the AFL-CIO's extensive international efforts to block the formation of a militant, independent workers' movement around the world. The AFL-CIO and its four institutes—the American Institute for Free Labor Development, African-American Labor Center, Asian-American Free Labor Institute, and Free Trade Union Institute—are supported by government funds and work in partnership with government agencies and private organizations. The result of this collaboration is a sophisticated effort to link international workers in a don't-rock-the-boat, pro-U.S., pro-business coalition that is unable to stand up to the power of transnational corporations.

"Building a force for international solidarity within the AFL-CIO is more urgent than ever. This Resource Center report will prove essential to this effort. It provides valuable information and analysis to a new generation of U.S. workers dissatisfied with their leaders." – Thad Russell, Labor Coalition on Central America

By Beth Sims. South End Press, 1992.
Paperback, 139 pages. ISBN 089608-429-9. $9.00

Resource Center Bulletin

UP-TO-THE-MINUTE RESEARCH AND ANALYSIS

Recent issues have featured articles on these critical topics:

Free Trade: The Ifs, Ands, & Buts is a 16-page overview of all the issues and terms in the free trade debate. Spring 1993, Nos. 31/32.

Global Capitalism, Global Unionism focuses on labor issues arising from the globalization of the U.S. and Mexican economies, and looks at some ways unions on both sides of the border have worked toward solidarity. Winter 1993, No. 30.

The Mexican Connection delves into the U.S.-Mexico drug problem, and how the United States is working in Mexico to stem the flow of narcotics and marijuana. Fall 1992, No. 29.

U.S. subscriptions: $5 year, $10 two years
Foreign subscriptions: $10 year, $20 two years
Back issues: $2 each postpaid
ISSN: 0891-2688

TO ORDER: *Shipping and handling charges within the U.S. are $3 for the first book, 50¢ for each additional. For shipment by ground to international locations, include $4 for the first book, $1.50 for each additional. Send check or money order to: Resource Center, Box 4506, Albuquerque, NM 87196. Order by phone using Visa/Mastercard: (505) 842-8288. Prices subject to change.*